FROM THE
HEART
OF SAINT
ALPHONSUS

FROM THE
HEART
OF SAINT
ALPHONSUS

EXCERPTS FROM
SAINT ALPHONSUS LIGUORI

EDITED BY NORMAN J. MUCKERMAN, C.SS.R.

Liguori
LIGUORI, MISSOURI

Imprimi Potest:
Richard Thibodeau, C.Ss.R.
Provincial, Denver Province
The Redemptorists

Published by Liguori Publications
Liguori, Missouri
www.liguori.org
www.catholicbooksonline.com

ISBN 0-7648-0837-0
Library of Congress Catalog Card Number: 2002102871

DEDICATION

*For the many fine Redemptorists
who have tried, by word and example,
to teach me the way of
Saint Alphonsus Liguori.*

–NORMAN J. MUCKERMAN, C.SS.R.

CONTENTS

FOREWORD BY THE EDITOR

It is almost incredible that Saint Alphonsus Liguori, living in a world that did not dream of word processors or even typewriters, wrote a hundred eleven books. Today in our own highly developed and highly educated world, there are people who have not even *read* that many.

Moreover, many of the books that Alphonsus produced were big, heavy, important tomes, some of them containing fifteen hundred or more pages, dealing with serious discussions on moral questions, church laws, and advice for the more spiritually minded. These books were all so well written, so solid, so important, that they earned for him the official title: Doctor of the Church.

There are other books written by Alphonsus which were designed more for popular consumption. These were books on such subjects as the necessity of prayer, how to prepare oneself for death and eternity, the glories of our Blessed Mother, and conformity to the will of God. These books, which won for Alphonsus the title "Doctor of Prayer," also became well known and widely read during his lifetime and even more so after his death in 1787. Throughout the years since then, more than twenty thousand editions of his writings have been published in over seventy languages. That is a record that even William Shakespeare does not possess.

One primary reason for his continued popularity is that Alphonsus always wrote in a simple style, a style that even the goatherds of his native southern Italy could understand and accept. He also wrote with warmth. He knew how to get into the hearts of his readers, as well as into their minds. He could do this, get into their hearts, that is, because he opened his own heart to them and let them see and sense his own passionate love for God.

Nowhere did he do this more than in his smaller works. These he wrote to tell readers about his own special, almost private, devotions. These shorter books contain a series of meditations for a particular feast, or about an important mystery. He always follows each meditation with a fervent prayer.

The book you are holding now, dear reader, contains four "novenas," devotions dear to the heart of Saint Alphonsus. They are a novena for Christmas, another novena for Pentecost, one more in honor of the Sacred Heart, and eight "considerations" (as he called them) for the Octave of Corpus Christi. Also included are Saint Alphonsus's reflections on the seven feasts of Our Lady, as well as his meditations in honor of Saint Joseph.

If "home is where the heart is," these warm and tender thoughts from Saint Alphonsus will show you where and how Alphonsus de Liguori lived.

—NORMAN J. MUCKERMAN, C.SS.R.
DECEMBER 25, 2001
FEAST OF THE INFANT JESUS

From the
Heart
of Saint
Alphonsus

Chapter One

NOVENA TO THE HOLY SPIRIT

INTRODUCTION

This novena consists of meditations and prayers to be used from the feast of the Ascension of Jesus into heaven until the feast of Pentecost. It is the most important of all novenas if only because it was the first ever to be observed and celebrated in the Church.

We learn this from the Acts of the Apostles. In chapter one of Acts we read that the apostles and our Blessed Lady, Mary the mother of Jesus, gathered in the upper room in Jerusalem on the evening of the day when Jesus ascended into heaven. There for nine days they devoted themselves to constant prayer (see Acts 1:14) until the first Pentecost Sunday.

Their gathering was marked by singular gifts and graces, principally by the gift of the Holy Spirit, the unique and most special blessing won for us by the passion, death, and resurrection of Jesus. This indeed was the promise Jesus made before his death when he told his disciples that if he did not die, he would not be able to send the Holy Spirit to them. "It is to your advantage that I go away, for if I do not go away, the Advocate will not come to you; but if I go, I will send him to you" (Jn 16:7).

Our holy faith tells us that the Holy Spirit is the love that the Father and the Eternal Word bear toward each other, and therefore the gift of love which Jesus imparts to us, and which is the greatest of all gifts, is especially attributed to the Holy Spirit. As Saint Paul wrote: "God's love has been poured into our hearts through the Holy Spirit that has been given to us" (Rom 5:5).

In this Novena to the Holy Spirit, we will consider above all the great value of divine love, so that we may desire before all else to obtain it for ourselves, and then endeavor, by means of pious actions and especially by prayer, to inundate ourselves in this love. Indeed, God has promised this gift to all who ask for it with humility. "If you, who are evil, know how to give good gifts to your children, how much more will the heavenly Father give the Holy Spirit to those who ask him!" (Lk 11:13).

—ALPHONSUS DE LIGUORI

THE SEQUENCE PRAYER
FOR PENTECOST SUNDAY

Come, Holy Spirit, come!
And from your celestial home
Shed a ray of light divine!
Come, Father of the poor!
Come, source of all our store
Come, within our bosoms shine.
You, of comforters the best;
You, the soul's most welcome guest;

Sweet refreshment here below;
In our labor, rest most sweet;
Grateful coolness in the heat;
Solace in the midst of woe.
O most blessed Light divine,
Shine within these hearts of ours,
And our inmost being fill!
Where you are not, we have naught,
Nothing good in deed or thought,
Nothing free from taint of ill.
Heal our wounds, our strength renew;
On our dryness pour your dew;
Wash the stains of guilt away;
Bend the stubborn heart and will;
Melt the frozen, warm the chill;
Guide the steps that go astray.
On the faithful, who adore
And confess you, evermore
In your sevenfold gift descend;
Give them virtue's sure reward;
Give them your salvation, Lord;
Give them joys that never end. Amen.
Alleluia.

MEDITATION I

Love Is a Fire That Inflames the Heart

Almighty God ordered his people, the Israelites, to keep a fire continually burning on his altar. "All night until the morning…the fire on the altar shall be kept burning" (Lev 6:9). Saint Gregory said that the altars of God are our hearts, and it is there that he wishes the fires of his eternal love to be always burning. This is the reason that the Eternal Father, not satisfied with having given us his Son Jesus, also wants to give us the Holy Spirit to dwell in us and keep us constantly on fire with his love.

Jesus himself affirmed that he had come into our world to inflame our hearts with the fire of love, and that he desired nothing more than to see this love burning brightly. "I came to bring fire to the earth, and how I wish it were already enkindled!" (Lk 12:49). Evidently after ascending into heaven Jesus forgot the injuries and ingratitude he had received on earth in order to send the Holy Spirit down upon us.

O most loving Redeemer, you seem to love us as much in your sufferings and shame as in your kingdom of glory. Was it for this reason, then, that the Holy Spirit chose to appear in the upper room in the form of tongues of fire? "There appeared to them tongues as of fire." Is it for this reason that the Church teaches us to pray: "May the Holy Spirit, we beseech you, O Lord, inflame us with the fire which Our Lord Jesus Christ came to cast upon the earth, and which he ardently desired to see enkindled"?

This indeed was the holy fire which has inflamed the saints

to do so many great things for God, to love their enemies, to deprive themselves of earthly treasures, to embrace with love torments and even death. Love does not remain idle, love never says "It is enough." For those who love, the more they do for God the more they want to do, and this in order to please him more and gain a greater share of his love.

This holy fire of love is fanned even more by mental prayer. As we read in Psalm 39:3: "While I mused, the fire burned." Therefore, if we desire to burn with love for God, let us love prayer, because prayer is the furnace in which divine love is enkindled.

Affections and Prayers

O my God, until now I have done little or nothing for you who have done so much for me. Because of my coldness toward you I deserve that you "vomit me out of your mouth." O Holy Spirit, I beg you to "melt the frozen, warm the chill," and enkindle within me an earnest desire to please you.

I renounce all my worldly gratifications and declare that I would rather die than give you the least displeasure. You appeared in the shape of fiery tongues. I consecrate my tongue to you, that I may never more offend you through it. You have given my tongue to me to praise you, and I have used it to offend you, and to draw others to sin against you. I repent of this with all my heart. Grant that from this day on I may honor you constantly by singing your praises, by frequently invoking your help, and by speaking of your goodness and infinite love.

I love you, O God of love! And you, Mary, most sweet spouse of the Holy Spirit, obtain for me this holy fire of love for God.

MEDITATION II

Love Is a Light That Illumines the Human Spirit

One of the saddest effects produced in us by the sin of Adam is the darkening of our intelligence because of physical passions which distort our reason. How unfortunate are those who allow themselves to be ruled by passion. Passion is a smoke-screen, a veil which prevents us from seeing the truth. How can anyone flee from evil if he or she does not know what evil is or where evil lies?

This darkening of the mind increases as our sins increase. But, fortunately, the Holy Spirit, whom we invoke as our "most blessed Light divine," not only inflames our hearts with love but also destroys our mental darkness by showing us the vanity of earthly goods and the value of heavenly treasures. This same Holy Spirit enables us to recognize the price of grace and the goodness of God, as well as the kind of love he deserves from us and the immense love he bears for us.

As Saint Paul writes: "Those who are unspiritual do not receive the gifts of God's Spirit, for they are foolishness to them, and they are unable to understand them because they are spiritually discerned." (1 Cor 2:14). The person who is absorbed in the pleasures of this world knows little of God's truths, with the result that he or she loves what should be shunned and hates what should be loved.

This is why Saint Mary Magdalene of Pazzi used to say about

God: "O Love not known! O Love not loved!" This is also why Saint Teresa taught that God is not loved because he is not known. And this is why so many other saints sought light from God by praying in the words of the psalmist: "Give light to my eyes, or I will sleep the sleep of death" (Ps 13:3), or "It is you who light my lamp; the LORD, my God, lights up my darkness" (Ps 18:28), or "Open my eyes, so that I may behold wondrous things out of your law" (Ps 119:18).

The truth is that without divine light we cannot avoid the dangers that lie in our path, nor can we easily find God.

Affections and Prayers

O Holy and Divine Spirit, I believe that you are truly God, one God with the Father and the Son. I adore you and acknowledge that you are the Giver of all the lights by which you have made known to me the evil I have done by offending you, and the obligation I have to love you above all things. I thank you for your gifts, and I repent of all my sins.

I have truly deserved that you should leave me in my darkness, but I see that you have not yet abandoned me. Continue then, O Holy Spirit, to enlighten me and make me know more and more your infinite goodness. Give me the strength to love you from now on with all my heart. Add grace to grace, so that I may be totally overcome by your grace and thus be forced to love none but you.

These favors I ask of you through the merits of my Savior, Jesus. I love you, my sovereign Good, and I pray that I will learn to love you more than myself. Please accept me and do not let me be separated from you again.

O Mary, my Mother, help me always by your prayers.

MEDITATION III

Love Is a Fountain That Satisfies Our Thirst

Love is also called a living fountain, a fire, and charity: "*Fons vivus, ignis, caritas*." Our Blessed Savior, speaking to the Samaritan woman, told her: "Those who drink of the water that I will give them will never be thirsty" (Jn 4:14). Love is the water that satisfies our thirst. Those who truly love God with their whole heart will neither seek nor desire anything else, because they find every good in God himself. So satisfied they are with God that they are able to cry out: "My Lord and my All! You, O God, are my entire good!"

But God can rightfully complain that many people go about seeking for fleeting and paltry pleasures from creatures, and forsake him who is their infinite good and source of all joy. "They have forsaken me, the fountain of living water, and dug out cisterns for themselves, cracked cisterns that can hold no water" (Jer 2:13).

For this reason God, who loves us and desires to see us happy, cries out: "Let anyone who is thirsty come to me" (Jn 7:37). Those who desire to be happy, says Jesus, let them come to me and I will give them the Holy Spirit who will make them blessed both in this life and in the next.

Jesus then goes on to say: "And let the one who believes in

me drink. As the scripture has said, 'Out of the believer's heart shall flow rivers of living water' " (Jn 7:38). Therefore, we may say that those who believe in Jesus and love him shall be enriched with so much grace that from their heart (that is, their will) shall flow many fountains of holy virtues. These fountains will not only preserve their own life, but will also give life to others.

The water of which Jesus speaks is the Holy Spirit, the gift of love which Jesus promised to send after his ascension, as we read in the same Gospel passage: "Now he said this about the Spirit, which believers in him were to receive; for as yet there was no Spirit, because Jesus was not yet glorified" (Jn 7:39).

The key which opens the flow of this blessed water is prayer, which obtains for us every good thing, according to the promise of Jesus: "Ask and you will receive" (Jn 16:24). We are indeed blind, poor, and weak creatures, but prayer gains for us light, strength, and an abundance of grace. Those who pray receive all that they wish. God desires to give us his graces, but he also wants us to pray for them.

Affections and Prayers

Lord, "give me this water." Lord, with the Samaritan woman I beseech you to give me this water of your love, which will make me be less concerned with things of this earth, and more concerned with living only for you, my loving Redeemer. "On our dryness pour your dew." My soul is dry and barren soil, producing nothing but the weeds and thorns of sin. Water it with your grace so that it may bring forth fruits for your glory before I leave this world.

O fountain of living water, O supreme good, how many times have I left you for the mudholes of this earth, in which I have polluted your gift of love. O, would that I had died before offending you. From now on, I will seek nothing but you, my God and Savior. Help me to be faithful to this resolve.

Mary, my Hope, keep me always under your protection!

MEDITATION IV

Love Is a Dew That Enriches Our Soul

Holy Mother Church teaches us to pray in these words: May the infusion of the Holy Spirit cleanse our hearts and enrich them by the internal sprinkling of his dew.

It is God's gift of love that like heavenly dew brings forth in us good desires, holy intentions, and good works. All these are the flowers and the fruits of the Holy Spirit.

Love is called a dew also because it cools the heat of bad passions and of temptations, as it is called in the Pentecost prayer: "Grateful coolness in the heat." This dew of love enters our heart especially in the time of prayer. A mere quarter of an hour's prayer is enough to mollify every feeling of hatred or intemperate love, however ardent it may be.

In the Scriptures we read: "He brought me to the banqueting house, and his intention toward me was love" (Song 2:4). This banquet hall is holy meditation, through which we receive God's love to help us love our neighbor as ourselves, and God above everything. The person who loves God loves prayer; and the person who does not love prayer will find it morally impossible to overcome his or her passions.

Affections and Prayers

O Holy Spirit, I will no longer live for myself, but I will spend the rest of my life loving and pleasing you. Therefore, I beg you to grant me the gift of prayer. Come down into my heart and teach me to pray as I ought. Give me the strength not to leave off prayer because I am tired, or because prayer becomes difficult. Give me also the grace to pray constantly, and to use those prayers which are most dear to your Sacred Heart.

Once I was lost because of my sins. But now I see, from all your loving kindness to me, that your will is for me to be saved and to become a saint. I desire for this to happen so that I may give you pleasure, and that I may love your infinite goodness more and more.

I love you, my sovereign Lord, my love and my all; and because I love you I give myself entirely to you.

And do you, Mary, my Hope, protect me always.

MEDITATION V

Love Is a Repose That Refreshes

In the Pentecost Sequence Prayer we read another role which the Holy Spirit plays in our life: "In our labor, rest most sweet," as well as being our "solace in the midst of woe." This Spirit of love is indeed a repose or rest that truly refreshes us, because the main purpose of love is to unite the will of the lover to that of the beloved. To the person who loves God then, there is comfort in every affront received, in every sorrow endured, in every loss suffered, because he or she recognizes that these trials and, in fact, all trials are part of God's will. Thus such a person finds peace and contentment in all tribulations merely by saying: "This is the will of God."

This is indeed the peace which surpasses all physical pleasures. As Saint Paul wrote: "And the peace of God, which surpasses all understanding, will guard your hearts and your minds in Christ Jesus" (Phil 4:7). This, too, is the reason that Saint Mary Magdalene of Pazzi was filled with joy when she said only the words: "The will of God."

In our life here on earth everyone must carry a cross. But Saint Teresa of Ávila says that the cross is heavy for those who drag it behind them, whereas for those who choose to embrace it, the cross is light. Our God knows how to strike and how to heal. As Job states: "For he wounds, but he binds up; he strikes, but his hands heal" (Job 5:18).

The Holy Spirit, by comforting and consoling us, can make every abuse and affliction sweet and pleasing. For this reason we should say in every and all adversity: "Lord, let this be done according to your holy will." And should we fear that some evil of this world might befall us, let us always say: "Lord, do whatever you will with me, for I will accept your will in all things."

It is a very good thing to repeat this offering of oneself frequently during each day, as was the practice of the great Saint Teresa of Ávila.

Affections and Prayers

O my God, how often have I opposed your will and even despised it for the sake of doing my own will. I regret this evil more than anything else. O Lord, from this day on I will love you with my whole heart. "Speak, LORD, for your servant is listening" (1 Sam 3:9). Tell me what you want me to do and I will do it. Your will shall be my only desire, my only love.

O Holy Spirit, help my weakness. You are goodness itself, how can I love any other than you. Draw all my affection to yourself by the sweetness of your holy love. I renounce everything in order to give myself entirely to you. Please accept me and help me.

And you, Mary my Mother, know that I trust in you also to help me.

MEDITATION VI

Love Is the Virtue That Gives Us Strength

As we read in the Scriptures: "Love is strong as death" (Song 8:6). Just as there is no earthly power that can overcome death, so there is no earthly difficulty which love cannot conquer. When there is a question of pleasing the beloved, love triumphs over all—losses, contempt from other people, even personal sorrow. Nothing is so complex or arduous that it cannot be made easy and clear by love.

There is one sure and certain sign by which we know if we

love God, and this is if we are as faithful in love in adversity as in prosperity. Saint Francis de Sales says that God is just as loving when he chastises us as when he consoles us, for he does everything to us out of love. Indeed, when God most sends suffering into our life that is when he loves us most. Saint John Chrysostom wrote that when Saint Paul was held captive in chains he was more fortunate than when he was taken in ecstasy into the third heaven.

For this reason the holy martyrs rejoiced and thanked God while in the midst of torments believing that the greatest favor that they could enjoy from God was having to suffer out of love for God. And other saints, when there were no tyrants to afflict or oppress them, became their own torturers, by the penances they inflicted upon themselves to please God. That is why Saint Augustine wrote that when a person loves, no task is too great to remain in that love, or else it become a labor of love.

Affections and Prayers

O God of my soul, I say that I love you, but what am I doing to prove my love? Nothing. This shows that either I do not love you, or that I love you too little. Send me, therefore, dear Jesus, the Holy Spirit that he may come and give me strength to suffer for your love, and to do something to show my love before I die.

O my beloved Redeemer, do not let me die cold and ungrateful as I have been in the past. Grant me the strength to love suffering. Come and dwell within my heart, take possession of it and make it entirely yours. I want to love you, my Lord, and if I really do love you I am assured, by Saint John himself, that you are already within me. "God is love, and those who abide in love abide in God, and God abides in them" (1 Jn 4:16).

Since therefore you are already with me, increase the flames, increase the chains, so that I may neither seek nor love anything else but you, and thus made one with you, may never be separated from you.

O Mary, my Queen and Mother, obtain for me the gifts of love and perseverance.

MEDITATION VII

Love Causes God to Dwell Within Us

The Holy Spirit is called "the soul's most welcome guest." This was the great promise made by Jesus to those who love him. "If you love me, you will keep my commandments. And I will ask the Father, and he will give you another Advocate, to be with you forever" (Jn 14:15–16).

The Council of Trent proclaimed that the Holy Spirit never leaves anyone as long as he is not driven away: "He does not forsake unless he be first forsaken."

God dwells in the person who loves him, but he also declares that he is not satisfied if we do not love him with our whole heart. Saint Augustine wrote that the Roman Senate would not admit Jesus into the circle of their gods, because they considered him to be a proud god, who would not allow another god to be accepted on the same level as himself. And this is true. Our divine Lord wants no rival to enter the heart of the person who claims to love him. When he sees that he is not the only object loved he is, so to speak, jealous. In his epistle Saint James writes: "Do you suppose that it is for nothing that the scripture says, 'God yearns jealously for the spirit that he has made to dwell in us'?" (Jas 4:5). In fact, Saint Jerome affirms: "Jesus is jealous." He does not wish that the world should share in our love which he desires to have all to himself, therefore he praises those who are his "spouses" by calling them enclosed gardens: "A garden locked is my sister, my bride, a garden locked, a fountain sealed" (Song 4:12). Yes, those who are God's lovers are gardens closed off from all earthly loves, a fountain sealed against worldly cares.

Should there be any doubt in our mind that Jesus deserves all our love? Not according to Saint John Chrysostom who says: "Jesus gave himself entirely to you, and left nothing for himself." Jesus has given you his blood and his life; there remains nothing more for him to give.

Affections and Prayers

O my God, I understand now that you wish me to be entirely yours. I have already so often driven you from me, but you have not refused to return to me in order to have me turn back to you. O my good God, please take possession of me entirely. Accept me, my Jesus, and do not let me ever live apart from you in the future.

Make it happen that as you seek me I in turn may continue to look for you for as long as you desire me. May I also desire nothing but you and your love.

Bind me to yourself, so that I may never more be separated from you.

Mary, my dear Mother, my Queen, I trust in you.

MEDITATION VIII

Love Is a Bond That Unites

The Holy Spirit, who is uncreated love and the indissoluble bond between the Father and the Eternal Word, is also the bond that unites us with God. "Love is the virtue," says Saint Augustine, "that unites us to God." For this reason, Saint Lawrence Justinian joyfully exclaimed: "O Love, your bond is so strong that it is able to bind even God, and unite him to us!" The bonds of the world are often chains of death, but the bonds of God are bonds of life and salvation because they unite us to God who is our true and only life.

Before Jesus came into the world, people turned from God and became attached to things of this world, refusing to unite themselves to their heavenly Creator and Father. But God, who is all love, has drawn them to himself by means of love, as he promised through the prophet Hosea: "I led them with cords of human kindness, with bands of love" (Hos 11:4).

These bands of love, of which our loving God speaks, are the blessings and inspirations which he pours into our life, the invitations and calls he offers and makes to us, the promises of Jesus our Redeemer, in the sacrifice of the Cross and in the sacrament of the altar, and finally the gift of the Holy Spirit.

The prophet Isaiah called out: "Loose the bonds from your neck, O captive daughter Zion!" (Isa 52:2). These words tell us that we are to let go of all earthly bondage, and unite ourselves to the Lord by the ties of holy love. "Above all, clothe yourselves with love, which binds everything together in perfect harmony" (Col 3:14).

This is why Saint Augustine was able to say: "Love, and do what you will." Love God, and you will surely come to understand that anyone who truly loves God will try to avoid causing him displeasure while at the same time seek to please him in all things.

Affections and Prayers

My dearest Jesus, how much have you done to oblige me to love you, and how much has it cost you to gain my love! I would truly be ungrateful if I loved you little, or divided my heart between creatures and yourself, especially after I see that you have given up your life and your blood for me.

From now on I resolve to detach myself from anything that could weaken or destroy my love for you. But you know that I am often weak in carrying out my good desires, and so I ask you, who have inspired me to make this resolution, to give me the strength to accomplish it.

My dearest Jesus, I desire you and you alone. Make me repeat this prayer continually in this life, and especially at the hour of my death. And you, my dear Mother Mary, obtain for me the grace that henceforth I may desire only God and his love.

MEDITATION IX

Love Is a Treasure That Contains Every Good

Love is that kind of special treasure to obtain which, as Scripture tells us, we must give up all other good things. "For it is an unfailing treasure for mortals; those who get it obtain friendship with God, commended for the gifts that come from instruction" (Wis 7:14). Love, then, makes us friends of God.

Saint Augustine asks: People, why do you go around seeking good things? Look only for the one good, namely, God himself, in which all other goods are contained. But we cannot find God who is this unique good if we do not give up earthly things. This is why Saint Teresa wrote: "Detach your heart from creatures, and you will find God."

The psalmist assures us that those who find God will discover everything their hearts desire: "Take delight in the LORD, and he will give you the desires of your heart" (Ps 37:4). Our human heart is always seeking the things that will make us happy; but if we look for them in creatures, no matter how many or how much we may acquire, we will never be satisfied. But if we seek God alone, he will satisfy all our desires.

Who are the happiest people in the world if not the saints? And why? Because they desire and search only for God.

There is a story told of a certain prince who went out hunting in the forest. There he met a hermit. The prince asked the hermit what he was doing in this solitary place. "And you," said the hermit, "what are you doing?" The prince replied: "I am here hunting wild beasts, but you didn't tell me as yet what you are doing here." The hermit replied: "I am here hunting for God."

When the wicked prince offered the hermit gold and other gifts if he would renounce God, the hermit sighed and said: "Are you asking me to give up God for a little dirt? What kind of exchange is this? Happy the person who knows how great a treasure God is, and seeks to obtain it, and it alone."

Saint Francis de Sales wrote: "When your house in on fire, all your treasures are thrown out of the window." And Father Paul Segneri, a great servant of God, used to say that love is a thief that robs us of all earthly affections so that we can truly say: "What else do I desire, my Lord, except you alone!"

Affections and Prayers

O my God, up till now I have not so much looked for you as for myself and my own pleasures, and for the sake of these pleasures I have turned my back on you, my sovereign good. But I take comfort in the words of your prophet Jeremiah: "The LORD is good to those who wait for him, to the soul that seeks him" (Lam 3:25).

My beloved Savior, I know the evil I have done in forsaking you, and I repent of this with my whole heart. I know that you are my infinite treasure. I will relinquish all and choose you for my only love. I desire you, and I sigh after you.

Come Holy Spirit and destroy in me by your sacred fire every affection which does not have you for its object. Grant that I may be all yours, and that I may overcome everything by pleasing you.

O Mary, my Advocate and Mother, help me by your prayers.

MEDITATION X

How We Can Love God and Become a Saint

The more we love God, the holier we become. Saint Francis Borgia says that prayer puts divine love into the human heart, while at the same time mortification removes from it earthly concerns and makes it more capable of receiving this holy fire.

The more that our heart is filled with worldly concerns, the less room it has for divine love. For this reason the saints have always tried to diminish their self-love and mortify their senses as much as possible. There are not too many saints, but as Saint John Climacus says we must live with the few if we are to be saved with the few. Saint Bernard wrote: "To be perfect, one must be singular," which means that to lead a perfect life, one must be unique, different from other people.

Above all, in order to become a saint it is necessary to desire and resolve to be a saint. Some people have the desire but they never go any further. The devil has no fear of these irresolute ones, says Saint Teresa, while adding that God is always a friend to the unselfish and great-hearted.

Sometimes the devil tries to make us think that it is a sign of pride if we wish to do great things for God. It would indeed be pride if we thought that we could do these great things on our own, trusting in our own strength. But it is not pride to resolve to become a saint when we trust in God and say along with Saint Paul: "I can do all things through him who strengthens me" (Phil 4:13).

We must then have courage, great resolve, and above all we must begin. Prayer can do everything for us. What we cannot do by ourselves, relying on our own strength alone, we can easily do with the help of God. God has promised to give us whatever we ask of him: "Ask for whatever you wish, and it will be done for you" (Jn 15:7).

Affections and Prayers

My dearest Redeemer, you ask for my love and command me to love you with my whole heart. Yes, my Jesus, I desire thus to love you, and I will profess that, trusting in your mercy, I will no longer fear because of my past sins. I now hate and detest them above every other evil, and I know that you forgive and forget the offenses of the repentant sinner who wants to love you.

Indeed, since I have offended you more than most other sinners, I will now try to love you more than most other people, relying on the help that I hope to receive from you. You want me to become a saint, and I want to be a saint to please you. For this reason I give myself to you entirely. Accept me, my loving Jesus, and make me all yours. Do not permit me to offend you further, but grant instead that I may give myself entirely to you as you gave yourself entirely to me.

O Mary, most loving and most beloved spouse of the Holy Spirit, obtain for me love and fidelity. Amen.

Chapter Two

NOVENA TO THE
SACRED HEART OF JESUS

INTRODUCTION

The best of all devotions is love for Jesus Christ, and the best way to develop that love is by meditating on the love which Jesus our loving Savior has shown for us and still offers us.

One holy writer is justifiably sad that so many people get involved in many other devotions while neglecting the practice of love for Jesus. The same complaint may be made about the many preachers and spiritual directors who talk about many things but speak little of love for our blessed Lord. This is not good, because love for Jesus Christ ought to be the principal, if not the only, devotion of a Christian. And at the same time, it is this love that preachers and confessors should be constantly recommending to their hearers and penitents so as to inflame them with love for our Redeemer.

This sort of neglect on the part of spiritual leaders is the reason that so many people make little progress in virtue, and thus remain in the same faults, and even at times relapse into serious sins. They are neither sufficiently urged nor admonished to develop a deeper love for Jesus, which is itself the golden cord that unites and binds them to God.

The basic reason for Jesus, the Eternal Word, coming into the world was to make himself loved. "I came to bring fire to the earth, and how I wish it were already kindled!" (Lk 12:49). This is why the Father sent his divine Son to us, so that he might make known to us God's love for us, and so obtain ours in return. Furthermore, Jesus promises that the Father will love us if we love him: "For the Father himself loves you, because you have loved me and have believed that I came from God" (Jn 16:27).

More than that, the Father gives us his graces when we ask for them in the name of the Son: "Very truly, I tell you, if you ask anything of the Father in my name, he will give it to you" (Jn 16:23). The Scriptures tell us that we are to become like Jesus and live in imitation of him: "For those whom he foreknew he also predestined to be conformed to the image of his Son" (Rom 8:29). But this can never happen if we do not meditate seriously on the love which Jesus has shown for us.

It was to further this kind of love and devotion that our Blessed Lord, as is related in the life of Saint Margaret Mary Alocoque, a Visitation nun, revealed to this holy religious his desire that in our own times the devotion and the feast of his Sacred Heart should be established and spread throughout the Church. Through this particular devotion to the Sacred Heart devout persons, by prayer and adoration, would especially be able to make reparation for the many abuses and injuries his loving heart receives, especially when it is exposed in the holy Sacrament of the Eucharist on the altar.

Later, Saint Margaret Mary, while she was praying before the Blessed Sacrament, received another revelation from Jesus who showed her his Sacred Heart surrounded by thorns, with a cross at its top, and on a throne of flames. As he did so, he said: "Behold the heart that has so much loved all people and has spared itself nothing for love of them, but has been so little loved by them."

Jesus went on to urge Margaret Mary to do all that she could to promote a special feast in honor of his Sacred Heart. This feast was to be celebrated on the first Friday after the Octave of the feast of Corpus Christi. There were three basic reasons for celebrating this feast: (1) that the faithful might give thanks for the great gift they received in the holy Eucharist; (2) that devout persons might, through this devotion, make reparation for the irreverences and insults Jesus receives in the Holy Eucharist; and (3) that they might also, through their devotion, make up for the lack of honor and respect in so many churches where Jesus is present but is so little recognized and adored.

At the same time, Jesus promised that he would send abundant graces on all who honored him through this special devotion, not only on the feast day itself, but on every day when they would visit him in the Most Holy Sacrament.

This devotion to the Sacred Heart of Jesus would be then nothing more than an exercise of love for our Savior himself. The principal focus of this devotion, the "spiritual" object, is the love with which the Heart of Jesus is burning for us his people, because love itself is generally attributed to the human heart. Even in holy Scripture is this stated, as witness these few examples: "My child, give me your heart" (Prov 23:26). Or:

"God is the strength of my heart and my portion forever" (Ps 73:26). Or again, "God's love has been poured into our hearts through the Holy Spirit that has been given to us" (Rom 5:5).

At the same time, the "material" (or sensible) object of this devotion is the most Sacred Heart of Jesus, not to be taken separately by itself but as united to his holy humanity, and thus to the divine Person of the Word.[1]

Saint Alphonsus wrote this introduction and composed this special novena in 1758. Seven years later in 1765, to Alphonsus's great joy, Pope Clement XIII gave permission to several churches in Europe to celebrate the feast of the Sacred Heart with a special Mass and with a proper Divine Office. From then on, it was only a question of time before the devotion to the Sacred Heart of Jesus spread ever more and more widely. Eventually the feast itself was elevated in rank to the highest order and is now solemnly celebrated by the Church worldwide.

---

1. Editor's note: In his introduction, Saint Alphonsus then goes into a somewhat long explanation of how and why this "new" devotion should to be both accepted and undertaken by devout people, in order that their devotion might help to hasten the official approval of the devotion by the Church. He also gives more details of the early history of the devotion and cites learned men of his time to support his argument that it is proper to center this devotion on the Sacred Heart. This is proper, says Saint Alphonsus, because the human heart, although it might not be the seat of affections and the principle of life, "is one of the primary fountains and organs of the life of man." Thus it can be maintained that the other parts of the body receive their principle of motion from the human heart, and that the heart has a major share in human affections.

MEDITATION I

The Loving Heart of Jesus

Those who wish to prove themselves lovable from every standpoint must of necessity make themselves loved. If we truly attempt to search out all the good qualities by which Jesus makes himself worthy of our love, we will—to our own good fortune—be constrained to love him. For among all hearts where is the heart that is more worthy of love than the Sacred Heart of Jesus?

His heart is all pure, all holy, and all full of love toward God and toward us. This is because he desires only the glory of the Father and our own good. His is the heart in which God finds all delight. Every perfection, every virtue, reign in the heart of Jesus. In it we find a most ardent love for God the Father, together with the greatest spirit of humility and respect possible. In it we discover a saving understanding of our sins which he has taken upon himself, united to the fullest confidence of a most loving Son. In it at the same time, we find a total abhorrence of our sins united to a deep recognition of our weaknesses. In it, too, we see a great sadness united to perfect conformity to the will of God.

In Jesus we find every quality that can be called attractive and lovable. Some people love others because of their beauty, or their innocence, or their ability to get along with others, or because of their unselfishness. But if there existed someone in whom these and all other virtues were united, would we be unable to love such a person deeply?

If we heard that in some foreign country there lived a prince or leader who was handsome, humble, courteous, kind, charitable, one who rendered good for evil, isn't it true that even though we might not ever get to know him nor he us, or that it would never even be possible for us to meet him, would we most likely take him to our heart, and fall in love with him? How is it possible, then, that Jesus, who has all these qualities to the most perfect degree and who loves us most tenderly, should be so little loved by so many people? How is it possible that we ourselves do not love him?

O my dear God, how does it happen that our divine Lord Jesus, who is the only one worthy of our fullest love, who has given us so many proofs of his love for us, cannot get us to love him? Why is it that we act as though he is not sufficiently worthy of our love? This is what caused some of the saints to weep, saints like Saint Rose of Lima, Saint Catherine of Genoa, Saint Teresa, and others, who seeing the ingratitude of so many people, cried out: "Love is not loved, love is not loved!"

Affections and Prayers

O my lovable Redeemer, what person more worthy of love could the Eternal Father command me to love than you yourself? You are the beauty of paradise, you are the love of your eternal Father, you are the throne of all virtues. O most lovable heart of Jesus, you deserve the love of all other hearts. Poor and wretched is the heart that does not love you.

My own heart has given you such a miserable response for so long a time as I have not truly loved you. Now, however, I no longer wish to reject your love, for I wish to love you forever. I will no longer forget you, because I do not wish to cause you to forget or forsake me. Do not allow this to happen to me, even though I deserve it.

O loving flames that burn in the heart of my Jesus, enkindle in my poor heart that holy fire which Jesus came down from heaven to light on earth. Consume and destroy all the impure affections that remain in my heart and prevent it from belonging entirely to you. If at one time I rejected and despised your love, now I wish to make you the entire object of my love. I love you and I wish to love none other than you. Show to your angels my heart, once afflicted by sin, but now burning with love for you.

Most holy Mother Mary, my hope, please assist me. Ask your son, Jesus, to make me, by his grace, all that he wants me to be. Amen.

Special Prayer of Saint Alphonsus to the Sacred Heart of Jesus

O loving heart of my Savior, you are the seat of all virtues, the source of all graces, the burning furnace of love which inflames the hearts of all who pray to you. You are the object of the Father's infinite love. You are the refuge of the afflicted, the haven of all who love you.

O sacred heart of Jesus, you are worthy of reigning over all other hearts, and of possessing the affection of all other hearts. O heart once wounded for me on the cross by the lance of my sins, you now remain continually present for me in the most Blessed Sacrament, wounded now by the lance of your own infinite love for me.

O loving heart of Jesus, you love us with so much tenderness and are so little loved by us in return. Heal my great ingratitude by inflaming my heart with a true love for you. Would that I could go all over the world to make known the graces, the sweetness, the goodness which you offer to those who love you! Please accept my deepest wish that I might see everywhere hearts burning with love for you.

O divine heart, be my consolation in trials, my comfort in anxieties, my strength in the storms of life. I consecrate myself to you, body and spirit, my life and my own heart, together with all that I am. I unite all my thoughts to your thoughts, all my affections to your affections, all my desires to your desires.

O Eternal Father, I offer to you the most pure love of the heart of Jesus. If you wish to reject my affections, you cannot reject those of your most holy Son. May his holy love make up for what is lacking in me, and render me pleasing in your sight. Amen.[2]

---

2. This prayer may be repeated every day of the novena.

MEDITATION II

How Much Jesus Loves Us

How difficult it is to understand fully the love that burns in the Sacred Heart of Jesus for us! He has loved us so much that if all people on this earth, plus all the angels and saints in heaven, were to unite their hearts and all their energies in one mountainous act of love, they could not equal even a thousandth part of the love which Jesus bears for us. He loves us infinitely more than we love ourselves.

He has loved us lavishly, superabundantly, to the extreme. In John 13:1 we read: "Having loved his own who were in the world, [Jesus] loved them to the end." What greater degree of love could there be than for a God to die for his creatures? Throughout all eternity there was never a moment when God did not think of us or love us. As he stated through the prophet: "I have loved you with an everlasting love" (Jer 31:3).

For love of us Jesus made himself man and chose a life of sufferings and a horrible death on the cross for our sake. He has loved us more than his own honor, more than comfort or repose, more than his own life, for he sacrificed everything to show us how much he loved us. Is not this kind of love sufficient to astound the angels of heaven for all eternity?

This immense love has also induced Jesus to remain with us in the Holy Sacrament as on a throne of love. He is present to us under the appearance of a small piece of bread, sometimes shut up in a tabernacle, where he seems to remain in a total annihilation of his divine majesty, without movement, and without the use of his senses—to such a degree that he seems to have no other duty than to love us. It is love that makes a lover desire to remain in the presence of his or her beloved; it is love that makes Jesus wish to reside with us in the Most Holy Sacrament.

It seems right to conclude that thirty-three years was not long enough a time for Jesus to spend with us on earth. No, in order to show his desire to be with us forever, he worked the greatest of all miracles, by instituting the Holy Eucharist. Note that the work of redemption was already done; the human race was already reconciled with the Father. Yet Jesus wanted to continue his presence among us in this sacrament because he could not bear to separate himself from us. As we read in the Scriptures, he [God] rejoices "in the inhabited world…delighting in the human race" (Prov 8:31).

Indeed, his love for us has induced him even to become our spiritual food, thus so uniting himself with us that his heart becomes one with our heart. "Those who eat my flesh and drink my blood abide in me, and I in them" (Jn 6:56). What a wonderful excess of divine love! One holy servant of God said this about the Eucharist: "If anything could shake my faith in the Eucharist it would not be a doubt as to how the bread could become flesh, nor how Jesus could be in several places at once, nor how he could be confined in so small a place, because in these concerns I would say that God can do everything. But if I were asked how God could love us so much as to make of himself our food, I can say only that this is a mystery of faith above and beyond my comprehension, and that the love of Jesus for us cannot be understood.

Affections and Prayers

O adorable heart of Jesus, heart so inflamed with love for us, heart created only to love us, how is it possible that you can be so unloved by us! O miserable creature that I am, I have also been one of those ungrateful ones who have not loved you. Forgive me, my Jesus, forgive my great sin of not having loved you enough. You are so lovable and so loving; what more could you have done to win my love!

I feel that because I have renounced your love I deserve to be condemned not to be able to love you at all. Dear Lord, chastise me in any way, but do not inflict this so great a punishment upon me. Grant me the grace to love you and then punish me as you will.

But how can I fear that you will punish me by not allowing me to love you when I remember your sweet command: "You shall love the Lord your God with all your heart, and with all your soul, and with all your mind" (Mt 22:37). Yes, Lord, you want to be loved by me and I will indeed love none but you, who have loved me so much.

O burning heart of Jesus, inflame my heart with love. Do not permit me in the future, even for a single moment, to live without your love. Rather, kill me, destroy me, do not let the world see such a spectacle of ingratitude as that I, who have been so loved by you, who have received so many favors and graces from you, should begin again to despise your love. I trust in the blood which you have shed for me that I will always love you and that you will always love me, that this our love will endure for all eternity.

O Mary, mother of fair love, you desire to see Jesus loved; unite me to him and never let me be separated from him or from you. Amen.

MEDITATION III

The Heart of Jesus Desires to Be Loved

Jesus does not need us. He is totally happy, totally comfortable, totally powerful with or without our love. Yet, as Saint Thomas Aquinas tells us, he loves us so much that he desires our love as much as if we were his God and as if his happiness depended on us. This is a truth that astonished holy Job: "What are human beings, that you make so much of them?" (Job 7:17).

Is it possible that God can want, and even eagerly ask for, the love of an insignificant creature? Merely allowing us to love him would have been too great a gift from God. But here we have Jesus, our Lord and our God, asking and even demanding our love: "My child, give me your heart" (Prov 23:26). And even if we try to drive him away, he stands outside the door of our heart and calls out to be let back in: "Listen! I am standing at the door, knocking" (Rev 3:20). He delights in being loved by us, and is greatly consoled when we repeatedly say to him: "My God, my God, I love you."

This attitude of Jesus is the result of the great love he bears for us. One who loves desires to be loved in return. Heart calls to heart; love seeks love. As Saint Bernard says: "Why does God love except that he himself be loved?" In this the saint echoes God's own statement: "So now, O Israel, what does the LORD your God require of you? Only to fear the LORD your God, to walk in all his ways, to love him, to serve the LORD your God with all your heart and with all your soul" (Deut 10:12).

This is the reason that Jesus tells us that he is the Shepherd who, after finding the sheep that was lost, calls all his neighbors to rejoice with him: "Rejoice with me, for I have found my sheep that was lost" (Lk 15:6). Jesus also tells us that he is like the father who, when his prodigal son returns from a far-off land and casts himself at his feet not only forgives him but embraces him warmly.

At the same time Jesus tells us that those who do not love him abide in death. "Whoever does not love abides in death" (1 Jn 3:14). But he likewise tells us that the Eternal Father accepts and welcomes those who love him: "God abides in those who confess that Jesus is the Son of God, and they abide in God" (1 Jn 4:15).

Will not all the above considerations, the invitations, the pleadings, the threats and the promises, move us to love God who desires so much to be loved by us?

Affections and Prayers

My dearest Redeemer, I will say to you with Saint Augustine, you command me to love you, and even threaten me with hell if I fail to do so. Yet what more fearful hell, what greater misfortune, can happen to me than to be deprived of your love! If then you wish to frighten me, you should tell me only that I will have to live without you, for this threat will cause me more fear than a thousand hells. For, as Saint Augustine concludes, if those condemned to hell could burn with love for you, hell itself would become a paradise, while on the contrary if the blessed in heaven could not love you, paradise would become hell.

I see, my dearest Lord, that because of my sins I have deserved to lose your grace, and to become incapable of loving you. However, I know that you still command me to love you, and I, at the same time, feel the desire to love you. This is another of your great graces. Therefore I ask for a further grace to do your will and to say, from the bottom of my heart, I love you, I love you, I love you.

Forget, dear Jesus, my past offenses. From now on, let us love one another forever. I will not leave you and you will not leave me. You will always love me, and I will always love you. I place all my hopes in you, and I ask you to make yourself loved totally and forever by a sinner who has offended you so much in the past.

O Mary, Immaculate Virgin, help me, pray to Jesus for me.

MEDITATION IV

The Sorrowful Heart of Jesus

It is impossible for us to appreciate how greatly afflicted the heart of Jesus was for love of us and at the same time not be filled with pity for him. Jesus himself confesses that his heart was so overwhelmed with sorrow that this alone would have been enough to make him die of grief had not his own divinity miraculously prevented this. He proclaimed this in the Garden of Olives: "I am deeply grieved, even to death" (Mk 14:34).

The principal sorrow affecting the heart of Jesus was not so much knowing the torments and insults his enemies were preparing for him. Rather, it was seeing how ready we would be to reject his immense love. Jesus distinctly saw all the sins which we would commit even after his sufferings, even after his bitter and ignominious death on the cross. He foresaw, too, the insults which sinners would offer his Sacred Heart which he would leave on earth in the Most Holy Sacrament as proof of his love. These insults are almost too horrible to mention: people trampling the sacred hosts underfoot, throwing them into gutters or piles of refuse, and even using them to worship the devil himself!

Even the knowledge that these and other defamations would happen did not prevent Jesus from giving us this great pledge of his love, the Holy Eucharist. Jesus has an infinite hatred for sin; yet it seems that his great love for us even overcomes this bitterness. Because of his love, he allowed these sacrileges to happen in order not to deprive us of this divine food. Should not this alone suffice to make us love a heart that has loved us so much?

What more could Jesus do to deserve our love? Is our ingratitude so great that we will still leave Jesus forsaken on the altar, as so many are wont to do? Rather, should we not unite ourselves to those few who gather to praise him and acknowledge his divine presence? Should we not melt with love, as do the candles which adorn the altars where the Holy Sacrament is preserved? There the Sacred Heart remains, burning with love for us. Shall we not in turn burn with love for Jesus?

Affections and Prayers

My dearest Jesus, behold at your feet one who has caused so much sorrow to your loving heart. How could I have hurt this heart which has loved me so much and has done everything possible to win my love? But now, dear Savior, be consoled because at long last my own heart has been touched by your grace and feels such deep sorrow for the sins I have committed against you that I could die of grief.

O holy heart of my Savior, grant me from this day forward such a horror of sin that I may indeed abhor even the slightest fault, by which I might displease you who certainly does not deserve to be offended by me. My Lord, I detest everything that offends you, and in the future I will love only you, and whatever you love. Give me the grace to call upon you constantly, and to repeat over and over again this prayer: My Jesus, give me your love, give me your love, give me your love.

And you, my dear Mother Mary, obtain for me the grace to pray to you constantly, asking you to make me love your son, Jesus.

MEDITATION V

The Compassionate Heart of Jesus

Where shall we ever find a heart more tender or compassionate than the Sacred Heart of Jesus? Where shall we find one that understands our afflictions as completely as this heart?

His sense of pity for us induced Jesus to come down from heaven to planet Earth. It also led him to call himself the Good Shepherd, come to give his life for us his sheep. At the same time, to obtain pardon for us of our sins, our compassionate Redeemer would not spare himself, but instead would sacrifice himself on the cross, to make satisfaction for the punishments we ourselves deserved.

This deep sense of pity and compassion leads Jesus to say to us as the Father said to Israel through the prophet Ezekiel: "Why will you die, O house of Israel? For I have no pleasure in the death of anyone, says the Lord GOD. Turn, then, and live" (Ezek 18:31–32). What our blessed Lord is telling us is that by separating ourselves from him we would be hastening our own eternal death. He does not want to see us lost, so we need not despair ever. Rather, we need to return and live.

The compassionate heart of Jesus compels him to tell us that he is that kind and loving father who embraced his prodigal son, even though that son rejected him and went off to a far-away land. Here in this tender story which Jesus himself related we discover a father who will not remember the hurts he received from his son. Ordinary men, even fathers, do not usually behave in this way, and even though they sometimes forgive, they cannot forget. Sometimes they even feel the need to seek revenge. And even if, because they fear God, they do not avenge themselves, they still do not feel inclined to continue their friendship with persons who have treated them badly.

O my Jesus, you pardon penitent sinners. You even give them everything in this world including your very self in Holy Communion. You give them everything in the next world as well, including eternal glory. You do not show even the slightest reluctance to being united for all eternity with someone who has offended you but who now is repentant. Tell me, where can we find a heart so lovable and compassionate as your Sacred Heart?

Affections and Prayers

O compassionate heart of my Jesus, have mercy on me. I say this now and I beg of you to give me the grace to say it always. Even before I offended you, my dear Redeemer, I did not deserve any of the many favors you have bestowed upon me. And after I offended you I certainly deserved to be abandoned by you and cast into hell. Because of your infinite compassion you have waited for me to repent, and have also preserved my life.

Because you have been so good to me in the past I now hope to remain always in your grace in the future. Give me then the light and the strength to be no longer ungrateful to you, or turn my back upon you ever again. No, my Jesus, now I love you and I will always love you. This is the mercy which I hope to receive from you. Never permit me to be separated from you again.

I beseech you also, my dear Mother Mary, keep me always close to your Son and to you. Amen.

MEDITATION VI

The Generous Heart of Jesus

One of the principal characteristics of good-hearted people is that they try to make everybody happy, especially those who are most afflicted and distressed. But where can we find a more good-hearted person than Jesus? He is infinite goodness, and for this reason he wishes more than anything to share his wealth with us: "Riches and honor are with me, enduring wealth and prosperity…. Endowing with wealth those who love me" (Prov 8:18, 21).

Saint Paul tells us that Jesus made himself poor that we might be rich: "For you know the generous act of our Lord Jesus Christ, that though he was rich, yet for your sakes he became poor, so that by his poverty you might become rich" (2 Cor 8:9). Thus it was that for this reason he chose to remain with us in the Holy Eucharist, where he lives with his hands full of graces so that, as Father Balthazar Alvarez writes, he might give them to those who visit him there. For this reason he gives himself to us totally in Holy Communion, to show us that he cannot refuse us any good gift, since he even gives himself whole and entire to us in this sacrament: "He who did not withhold his own Son, but gave him up for all of us, will he not with him also give us everything else?" (Rom 8:32).

Truly, in the holy heart of Jesus we receive every good, every grace desirable. "I give thanks to my God always for you because of the grace of God that has been given to you in Christ

Jesus, for in every way you have been enriched in him…so that you are not lacking in any spiritual gift as you wait for the revealing of our Lord Jesus Christ" (1 Cor 1:4–5, 7). See how much we owe to God! We are indeed debtors to him for so many graces: the grace of redemption, of light, of pardon, of vocation, as well as the grace to resist temptations, or to bear contradictions patiently. With the help of God we can do nothing good whatsoever: "Apart from me you can do nothing" (Jn 15:5).

What is more, says our loving Savior, if in the past you have not received even more graces, do not complain, but blame it on yourself. You it was who neglected to ask me, says the Lord. "Until now you have not asked for anything in my name. Ask and you will receive" (Jn 16:24).

Oh, how rich and generous is the Sacred Heart of Jesus— "generous to all who call on him" (Rom 10:12). All those who are serious in asking grace and help from the Lord receive mercy and aid. As the psalmist wrote: "For you, O LORD, are good and forgiving, abounding in steadfast love to all who call on you" (Ps 86:5). Let us, therefore, go always to this Sacred Heart, asking with total confidence, and we shall receive whatever we ask for.

Affections and Prayers

Ah, my Jesus, you have not refused to give up your blood and your life for me, and shall I refuse to give you my miserable heart? No, my dear Redeemer, now I offer it entirely to you. I give you my will; please accept it and dispose of it according to your pleasure.

I can do nothing, I have nothing. But I do have the heart which you have given to me, and which no one can take from me. Others may take from me my possessions, even my blood, but they cannot take my heart. With it I can love you, and with it I will love you. Teach me then, dear Jesus, how to forget myself and how to love you. I am determined to love you, but to do this I need your help. Make this heart of mine entirely yours. In the past I have been ungrateful and unfaithful, and so through my own fault I have been deprived of your love. Do not let this happen anymore, but rather cause my heart to be all on fire for love of you.

O my loving Savior, grant that from this day forward, I will accept your holy will as the rule of all my actions, all my thoughts, all my desires. I trust that you will give me the grace to fulfill this resolve which I make before and in submission to your loving Heart.

Mary, whose own immaculate heart was always and entirely united to the heart of your Son, obtain for me the grace to live in the future entirely according to God's holy will. Amen.

MEDITATION VII

The Grateful Heart of Jesus

Our Blessed Lord, in and through his Sacred Heart, is so grateful that he cannot observe the most trifling act done for love of him, or hear the simplest word spoken for his glory, or even recognize one single good thought directed toward pleasing him, without bestowing some kind of reward. And his rewards are always superabundant—even a hundredfold!

When we human beings show our gratitude for something good done to us, we do it and get it over with. We fulfill our obligation, as it were, and then think no more about it. Jesus does not act that way with us. He not only rewards us a hundred-fold in this life for any good action we perform for him, but he also compensates us infinitely throughout eternity. Who of us, then, would be so careless as to neglect doing all that we can to please his most grateful heart?

In point of fact, how can anyone fail to recognize the infinite graciousness of our Savior? If Jesus had shed only a single drop of blood, or even only one tear, for our salvation, we would owe him infinite gratitude. After all, one drop of his blood, one tear from his eye, would have had infinite value in the sight of his Eternal Father and would have won for us infinite grace. But Jesus gave up his entire life for us. He gave us all his merits, he offered up for us all his sufferings, he shed all his blood for us, he accepted all the reproaches heaped upon him in our stead. Should we not, then, be under an infinite obligation to love him with a most grateful heart?

Think of it! We have no trouble showing our gratitude to others, even to animals. If a little dog shows us any sign of affection, we pet and pat it, we even reward it with special treats. How, then, can we fail to show our gratitude to Jesus our loving Savior? How can we think of rejecting his love, or even disobeying him instead?

Affections and Prayers

O my beloved Jesus, here I am at your feet. I am an ungrateful sinner, grateful to others but not to you, who have even died for me to oblige me to love you. But the knowledge that I am dealing with one who is infinite in mercy, one who has a heart full of goodness, one who proclaims that he forgives all repentant sinners, consoles me, and gives me courage.

My dearest Jesus, in the past I have offended you, but now I wish to love you more than everything, more than myself. Tell me what you wish me to do, for I am ready to do anything with your help. I believe that you have created me, that you have died for me, that for my sake your remain with me in the Blessed Sacrament. I thank you for all this, and wish to love you more and more. O, bind me, unite me to your most Sacred Heart.

Mary, my dearest Mother, never let me again be ungrateful to your son, Jesus. Pray for me. Amen.

MEDITATION VIII

The Unloved Heart of Jesus

There is no greater sorrow for a loving heart than to see its own love rejected and despised. This is all the more true when the proofs of this love are so strong, and when the rejection stems from ingratitude.

If we as creatures of God should renounce all our goods, go

out into some abandoned place, live there, eat only wild foods, sleep on the bare earth, do penance by scourging ourselves to the point of drawing blood, and finally be killed for the sake of Jesus Christ, would all this ever be a fitting compensation for what Jesus, by his sufferings and death, has done for us? And if we would continue to sacrifice ourselves every moment until our death, would this equal even in the smallest degree the love that Jesus has shown us by giving us himself in the Most Holy Sacrament? Just try to invent or dream up something similar to a God concealing himself under the form of bread in order to become the spiritual food for his creatures!

But, sad to say, see what small amount of gratitude people show to our blessed Lord, what sort of reparation do they make to Jesus for what he has done and still does for them! How poorly they treat him, how forgetful they are of his laws, his counsels, his inspirations! Sometimes they treat him worse than people treat their enemies, their servants, or even the greatest scoundrels on earth.

Can we, who profess to love Jesus, think of all the injuries which Jesus has received and still receives every day and not feel the deepest sorrow for him? Should we, who claim to be his followers, not try by our own love to recompense the infinite love of his Sacred Heart, which remains on earth in the Most Holy Sacrament, inflamed with the same love for us? This is the same Jesus who is anxious to give us every good gift, to give himself entirely to us and to receive us into his heart whenever we go to him. "Anyone who comes to me I will never drive away" (Jn 6:37).

How often we have heard or read the story of how God created the world for us, or of how Jesus was born in a stable, how he died on the cross, and rose from the dead for us. My God, if we met any other person who had conferred on us any single one of these blessings, we could not help loving him! It seems that only God has this kind of misfortune, that no matter what he does to make us love him, we do not respond in kind. Instead of being loved, our blessed Lord is neglected and even at times despised. People, sad to say, forget how much God loves them.

Affections and Prayers

O Sacred Heart of Jesus, abyss of mercy and love, how is it that when I see your goodness toward me and my own ingratitude toward you, I do not die of sorrow? You have given your life for me, and even more, you sacrifice yourself anew every day for me in the Holy Eucharist. O my good God, how can I be so ungrateful to you! Put an end to my ingratitude by wounding my heart with your love and making me entirely yours. Do not let me forget your many sufferings for me.

Even though you have seen how ungrateful and unworthy of your love I have been in the past, you did not cease to love me. How much more will you love me now that I am determined to love nothing but you, and desire nothing else than to be loved by you. Grant that this day may be the day of my total conversion, so that I may begin to love you as you deserve, and never cease loving you in the future. Make me die to everything but you, in order that I may live entirely in you and for you, always burning with love for you.

Mary, your immaculate heart was the blessed altar that was always on fire with divine love. Make my heart like yours. Obtain this grace for me from your Son who delights in honoring you, by denying nothing you ask of him. Amen.

MEDITATION IX

The Faithful Heart of Jesus

Oh, how faithful is the beautiful Sacred Heart of Jesus toward those whom he calls to his love. As Saint Paul himself tells us: "The one who calls you is faithful" (1 Thess 5:24).

This faithfulness on God's part is more than enough to make us hope for all things from our loving Lord, even though we deserve nothing. If we have unfortunately driven God from our heart, then let us now open the door to him, and he will enter immediately, just as he promised: "Listen! I am standing at the door, knocking; if you hear my voice and open the door, I will come in to you and eat with you, and you with me" (Rev 3:20).

If we wish for graces, let us then ask God for them in the name of Jesus, for he has promised to give them to us. "Very truly, I tell you, if you ask anything of the Father in my name, he will give it to you" (Jn 16:23). And if we feel tempted, let us trust in the merits of Jesus, for the Father has promised that he will not permit our enemies to tempt us beyond our strength. "God is faithful, and he will not let you be tested beyond your strength" (1 Cor 10:13).

How much better it is to deal with God than with people. How often people promise things, and then fail to deliver, either because their promises are only lies, or because, having promised us something, they change their minds. God tells us as much in the Scriptures: "God is not a human being, that he should lie, or a mortal, that he should change his mind" (Num 23:19). God can never be unfaithful to his promises because he is all truth, and cannot possibly lie to us. Nor can he change his mind, because whatever he wills is just and right. God has promised to receive all who come to him, to give them help when they ask for it, and to love those who love him, and he will keep his promises!

Would that we were as faithful to God as he is to us. How often, in times past, have we promised to love God, to serve God, to belong to God, and then have failed to do so, or have been unfaithful. Today let us beg God to give us the strength to be faithful to our promises, and to be faithful to Jesus in the few things which he asks us to do. He will be totally faithful in rewarding us with heaven and all that heaven brings. He will say to us what the master said to the faithful servant: "Well done, good and trustworthy slave; you have been trustworthy in a few things, I will put you in charge of many things; enter into the joy of your master" (Mt 25:21).

Affections and Prayers

Oh, my dearest Redeemer, would that I had been as faithful towards you as you have been to me. Whenever I opened my heart to you, you have entered in, to forgive me and to take me back into your love. And whenever I called upon you, you have hurried to help me. Despite your loving faithfulness, I have been fickle and disloyal. I have promised you my love and then many times have taken it back, as if, O

Lord, you did not deserve it, or that you were less worthy of it than the creatures on whom I have bestowed it.

Forgive me, my Jesus. I am sorry for my great ingratitude. Have pity on me and do not permit me to forsake you again. Inflame my miserable heart, so that it may burn with love for you as your Sacred Heart burns with love for me. Make me love you with all my strength, so that I will remain faithful to you until death. I ask for this grace, along with the greater grace of always praying for it. Grant that I may die rather than ever betray you again.

Mary, my dear Mother, help me to be faithful to your Son. Amen.

Chapter Three

MEDITATIONS FOR THE OCTAVE OF CORPUS CHRISTI

MEDITATION I

The Love of Jesus in the Most Holy Sacrament

Our most loving Redeemer realized full well that once he had accomplished our redemption by his death and resurrection he would return to heaven. Indeed, he was especially reminded of this when he drew near to the hour of his death. As Scripture tells it: "Jesus knew that his hour had come to depart from this world and go to the Father" (Jn 13:1). He did not wish to leave us alone in this valley of tears, so he gave us one more gift. It was the gift of his very own self, present in the Most Holy Sacrament, the Holy Eucharist.

Saint Peter of Alcantara once wrote that no tongue on earth would be able adequately to express the greatness of the love that Jesus has for each and every one of us. And he also pointed out that Jesus, at the time when he was about to leave this earth, and not wishing that his absence would lead us to forget him, gave us a living memorial of himself. So he left us himself in the Blessed Sacrament, a sacrament of love by which he would remain with us until the end of time. "I am with you always, to the end of the age" (Mt 28:20).

Our holy faith tells us that we may find him as a prisoner of love in as many tabernacles as exist in the world. He is present in the Eucharist for all who seek him. Saint Bernard once objected: "But Lord, this is not compatible with your divine dignity!" And Jesus responded: "It is enough that it is compatible with my love."

Many pilgrims go to the Holy Land to visit and pray at the sites which were part of the life and death of Jesus on earth. In their piety, they go to the cave in Bethlehem, the courtyard where Jesus was condemned, the hall where he was scourged, the hill of Calvary where he died, the grave in which he was buried. But how great should be our emotions when we visit an altar where Jesus remains in the Most Holy Sacrament! The Venerable Father John Ávila used to say that of all the shrines and sanctuaries in the world none is more beneficial or more sacred than a church where Jesus is present in the Holy Eucharist.

Affections and Prayers

O my beloved Jesus, you have loved us with such an excessive love! What more could you do to make yourself loved by us who are so ungrateful? If we really loved you, we would be constantly filling all of our churches thanking you and burning with love for you, especially since we would recognize you present there in the Eucharist.

But we are so forgetful of you and your infinite love
for us. We are ready enough to please other people,
especially if from them we might expect some
worldly gift or advantage. But we so often leave you
abandoned and alone. Oh, that I might make reparation for such ingratitude by my devotion to the Holy
Eucharist!

My Redeemer, I am sorry that I have been so careless and ungrateful in the past. Now and in the future
I will try not to be so any longer. I will live only to
love you and to serve you as much as I possibly can.
You deserve the love of all hearts, and certainly all
of my love. If I have not loved you enough in the
past, now I desire nothing but to love you, my God
and my all.

Most holy virgin Mary, obtain for me a great love
for the most blessed Sacrament. Amen.

MEDITATION II

Jesus Remains on the Altar,
So That Everyone May Be Able to Find Him.

Saint Teresa of Ávila wrote that in her world and during her
lifetime, it was virtually impossible for anyone to speak to a
ruler or a king. The most they could hope for, especially if they
were poor, was to have an intermediary speak for them. But
when we want to converse with you, O King of heaven, no third
person is needed. Anyone and everyone who wishes to talk with
you can find you in the Most Holy Sacrament of the altar and

speak with you freely and without restriction or delay. It was for this reason, Saint Teresa adds, that Jesus in the Holy Eucharist has hidden his divine majesty under the appearance of bread for in this way he gives us more confidence and removes from us all sense of fear.

From the tabernacle Jesus cries out, as he did while he was here on earth: "Come to me, all you that are weary and are carrying heavy burdens, and I will give you rest" (Mt 11:28). Come, says Jesus, all you who are poor. Come all you who are sick or afflicted. Come all of you, whether you are sinner or saint. Come and you will find in me a remedy and a cure for all your sufferings and woes, for all your ills.

Jesus desires to console and help all who turn to him; that is why he is present at all hours of the day and the night, so that he may be there for everyone, and so that he might give everyone whatever grace or gift is needed or requested.

Saints and other holy people understand this. Their greatest pleasure in all the world is to remain in the presence of Jesus in the blessed Sacrament. Entire nights, entire days, seem to them as mere moments, precious moments. One Poor Clare nun was asked what she did while remaining for so long a time before the tabernacle. She answered with surprise: "What do I do there? Why, I thank, I love, and I pray." And Saint Philip Neri, while in the presence of his eucharistic Lord, would repeat over and over again: "Behold my love! Behold all my love!"

If we could learn to love Jesus in the Eucharist as these holy people did, then days and nights spent in his presence would seem like short moments to us.

Affections and Prayers

O my sweet Jesus, I hope that from now on whenever I visit you in the Blessed Sacrament I will say with Saint Philip Neri: "Behold my love, behold all my love!" Yes, my Redeemer, I wish to love none other than you; I want you to be my only love.

I feel that I should die of sorrow when I remember how often in the past I have loved creatures and my own pleasures more than you, or how I have turned my back on you. But you did not want me to be lost, and so you have so patiently borne with my lack of love. Instead of punishing me, you have pierced my heart with so many darts of love that I can no longer resist your advances.

I see now that you want me to give myself entirely up to you. But for this to happen, you must help me to detach my heart from all earthly affections and from myself. Grant that I may seek none other than you, that I may think of none other than you, that I may speak of none other than you. Grant also that I may seek to live and die for you alone.

O my Jesus, come and occupy my whole heart and soul; drive out from me all other loves, so that I may love you in the most Holy Sacrament and recognize you as my God and my All.

Mary, my hope, pray for me and make me belong entirely to Jesus. Amen.

MEDITATION III

The Great Gift We Receive From Jesus Who Gives Us Himself in the Holy Eucharist

The tremendous love which Jesus has for us forced him to do even more than die an ignominious death on the cross. To prove even further his love for us, and to oblige us to love him even more in return, our blessed Lord left us himself in the Holy Eucharist. He did this on the very last night of his life on earth, when he gave us his entire self in this Blessed Sacrament.

God, we know, is omnipotent. He can do all things. Yet, after giving us himself in this sacrament of love which we call the Holy Eucharist, he is unable to do anything more for us. As the Council of Trent declared, in giving himself to us in Holy Communion, Jesus pours out all the riches of his infinite love in this one gift.

Saint Francis de Sales writes: How honored would a lowly servant feel if his lord and master, while at table, gave him a portion of his own meal! Even more, what if this portion would be a piece torn out of his own arm? Jesus in Holy Communion gives us not just a part of his own meal, not just a portion of his own flesh, but his entire body! "Take, eat; this is my body" (Mt 26:26).

And we should note also that together with his whole body he gives us also his soul and his divinity, so that, as Saint John Chrysostom says, our blessed Lord thus gives us all that he has. Nothing more remains for him to offer us. "He gives everything to us and leaves nothing for himself."

O wonderful generosity of divine love, that our God, who is Lord of all, makes himself entirely ours!

Affections and Prayers

O my Jesus, what more can you do to make us love you? Please make us understand your excess of love in reducing yourself to food so that you can be united with us who are poor sinners. You love us so much that you do not refuse to come to us again and again in Holy Communion. And yet, I have again and again driven you away from me by my sins.

But, dear Lord, I know now that you do not despise a humble and contrite heart. You became man for us, you died on the cross for me, and now you give yourself to me as my spiritual food. What more can you do to gain my love?

I declare now that I am sorry. I could die with grief for having so often offended you. And now, through your grace, I repent with all my heart for my many sins. I want to love you above all things. I desire nothing more than to love you. My only fear is to live without your love.

My beloved Jesus, do not in the future refuse to come into my heart. I would rather die than drive you away again. I promise to do all that I can to please you. Come and inflame my soul with your love.

Mary, my Mother, pray for me and by your prayers make me grateful for the wonderful love your son, Jesus, has shown for me. Amen.

MEDITATION IV

The Great Love Which Jesus Shows Us in the Blessed Sacrament

"Now before the festival of the Passover, Jesus knew that his hour had come to depart from this world and go to the Father. Having loved his own who were in the world, he loved them to the end" (Jn 13:1). Jesus desired to give us the greatest possible pledge of his affection: the gift of the Most Holy Sacrament. Saint John Chrysostom interprets the words "he loved them to the end" to mean that he loved them "with extreme love."

Let us note also the time when Jesus instituted this great Sacrament. It was on the night preceding his own death. Saint Paul explains what happened in these words: "For I received from the Lord what I also handed on to you, that the Lord Jesus on the night he was betrayed took a loaf of bread, and when he had given thanks, he broke it and said: 'This is my body that is for you. Do this in remembrance of me'" (1 Cor 11:23–24).

At the very same hour when wicked men were preparing to put him to death, Jesus gave them (and us) the last proof of his love. We are genuinely and deeply impressed by any sign of affection our friends offer to us at the time of their own sickness and death. This was the reason, we may conclude, that Jesus bestowed the Eucharist as a gift of his love just before his own death. This is also the reason that Saint Thomas Aquinas called the Eucharist "the sacrament of love, and the pledge of the highest love." It is also why Saint Bernard declared it "the love of loves." In this Holy Sacrament our Blessed Lord unites all the many other acts of love he has done for us.

No wonder, then, that Saint Mary Magdalene of Pazzi named the first Holy Thursday "the day of love"!

Affections and Prayers

O infinite love of Jesus, so worthy to be loved by us! Yet how is it that even though we see how much you have loved us we still love you so little? Is there anything more that you could do to make us love you more?

When shall I love you as you have loved me? O my Jesus, show me more and more the greatness of your mercy so that I may burn more and more with love for you, and seek to please you always.

Alas, there was a time when I did not love you at all, and even despised your grace and your love. But now, I am reassured by the fact that I am truly sorry for this, and I can truly hope for pardon since you have promised to forgive those who repent.

Help me, my Savior, through the merits of your passion; help me to love you with my whole heart and soul, and with all my strength. Oh, that I could die for you as you have died for me!

Mary, my Mother, obtain for me the grace henceforth to love my God above all things. Amen.

MEDITATION V

Our Union With Jesus Through the Holy Eucharist

Saint Denis says that the principal effect of love is achieving union. This is the reason that Jesus instituted the Holy Eucharist: to become totally united to us. He had already given himself to us as our blessed Lord, our example, and our victim. There remained for him only to give himself to us as our food. He would become united with us just as food when eaten becomes one with the person who partakes of it.

In this regard Saint Bernardine of Siena wrote: "The full and final extent of Jesus' love was shown when he gave himself to be our food. Thus he was willing to be united with us in every way, just as food and the one who eats it become mutually one." It was not enough for Jesus to become one with us in assuming our human nature; he also, through this Holy Sacrament, found a way to become one with us as individuals through Holy Communion.

Saint Francis de Sales comments on this in these words: "In no other act that Jesus performed can he be seen as more loving or more tender toward us than in the Eucharist where he in a sense annihilates himself and reduces himself to food. Thus he enters the hearts of his faithful people."

The love which Jesus has for us leads him, as Saint John Chrysostom wrote, to merge himself with us, to fuse himself with us in such a way that we might become one with him, just as united as are those who love deeply. He wills that his heart and our heart should form one heart.

Jesus himself said as much while still on earth: "Those who eat my flesh and drink my blood abide in me, and I in them" (Jn

6:56). The union which Jesus speaks of is not one of mere affection, but a true and real union. Saint Cyril of Alexandria explains it this way: just as two candles will melt together to make one, so the person who receives the Holy Eucharist becomes one with Jesus.

Let us imagine, then, that when we receive Holy Communion Jesus is saying to us what he said to his servant, Margaret of Ypres: "See, my daughter, the beautiful union which now exists between you and me; come then and love me, and let us remain forever united in love, and never be separated again."

Affections and Prayers

O my dear Jesus, this is precisely what I ask now and always when I receive you in Holy Communion: "Let us remain forever united in love, and never be separated again." I know that you will not separate yourself from me, if I do not first separate myself from you. My fear, however, is that I should break away from you by sin, just as I have done in the past.

O my Redeemer, do not allow this to happen. "Never permit me to be separated from you." As long as I am alive, I live in danger of this happening. Therefore, I beseech you, through the merits of your own death, let me die rather than repeat this great injury to you. May I repeat this prayer always, over and over again: "Never permit me to be separated from you."

O Mary, Mother of mercy, pray for me now; obtain for me the grace never more to be separated from Jesus, your Son and my Savior. Amen.

MEDITATION VI

How Deeply Jesus Desires to Become One With Us Through Holy Communion

"Jesus knew that his hour had come" (Jn 13:1). This hour which Jesus called "his" was that hour on the very night when his passion was to begin. Why, we may ask, did our Savior call such a sad and painful hour "his hour"? It was because this was the hour which he had looked forward to, and even sighed for, during his entire life. It was the hour and the night on which he was determined to leave himself to those he loved under the form of the Holy Eucharist, and for whom he was to suffer and die on the cross.

Recall the very touching words he used on that momentous occasion: "I have eagerly desired to eat this Passover with you before I suffer" (Lk 22:15). These words speak to us of his desire and even eagerness to unite himself to us in the Sacrament of love. Saint Laurence Justinian, noting that these words came from the very heart of Jesus burning with love, wrote: "This is the voice of a most passionate love."

This same fiery love which burned then in the heart of Jesus is aflame today. What is more, Jesus offers us today the same invitation to receive him as he gave to his disciples: "Take, eat; this is my body" (Mt 26:26). To encourage us further to receive him with all our love he even promises us heaven: "Those who eat my flesh and drink my blood have eternal life" (Jn 6:54). And those who refuse to receive him are threatened with death: "Very truly, I tell you, unless you eat the flesh of the Son of Man and drink his blood, you have no life in you" (Jn 6:53).

These invitations, these promises, and even these threats all arise from the great desire which Jesus has to unite himself to us through Holy Communion, a desire which springs from the deep love he has for us. Speaking one day to Saint Mechtilde, our blessed Lord said: "There is no bee which seeks to draw honey out of flowers with more eagerness and delight than I have to enter into the hearts of those who desire to receive me." It is because Jesus loves us so much that he wants us to love him so much. And it is because he so strongly desires the love of our hearts that he wants to give us his love. Saint Gregory wrote: "God thirsts to be thirsted after." Blessed are those who approach Holy Communion with a great desire to be closely united to Jesus.

Affections and Prayers

My loving Jesus, you can give us no greater proofs of your love than those which you have already given us. You have given your life for us. You have even bequeathed yourself to us in holy Communion, that we may be nourished with your own flesh and blood. You urge us to receive your own body and blood in this sacrament.

How can we see all these testimonies of your love and fail to love you in return? O loving Lord, do not allow me to continue to live ungrateful for your great goodness to me. I thank you for giving me the time and opportunity not only to regret the offenses I have committed against you, but also to love you for the rest of my life.

Help me, my Jesus, to reject and expel from my heart each and every affection which is not directed toward you, so that from this day forward I may not desire, nor seek, nor love anyone but you alone. My God, whom shall I love if not you, who are my supreme good.

Mary, my dearest Mother, take my heart into your keeping and fill it with pure love for Jesus. Amen.

MEDITATION VII

Holy Communion Obtains for Us the Grace of Perseverance

When Jesus comes to us in Holy Communion, he brings us every grace, and especially the grace of final perseverance. In fact, the principal effects of this spiritual food are to nourish us spiritually, and to give us more strength, not only in our efforts to reach perfection but also in our efforts to resist those enemies who desire our spiritual death.

This is why Jesus calls himself in this sacrament our heavenly bread. "I am the living bread that came down from heaven. Whoever eats of this bread will live forever" (Jn 6:51). Just as earthly bread sustains our physical life, so this heavenly bread ensures our spiritual life by helping us to persevere in God's love.

The Council of Trent taught that Holy Communion is the medicine which frees us from daily faults and preserves us from committing serious sin. Pope Innocent III wrote that through his passion Jesus delivered us from sins already committed, while through the Eucharist he protects us from possible future sins.

This is the reason, says Saint Bonaventure, that we must not abstain from Holy Communion because we sinned in the past. Rather, says the saint, it is for this very reason we should receive this sacrament more frequently in the future. The more infirm a person feels, the more he or she needs a doctor.

Affections and Prayers

O dear Lord, I am such a miserable sinner and as such I sincerely regret my many weaknesses and my many falls from grace. And how could I have ever resisted sin while staying away from you who are my strength? If I had gone more often to you in Holy Communion, I would not have been so often overcome by my enemies.

But do not let this happen again, either now or in the future. I will say with the psalmist: "In you, O LORD, I seek refuge; do not let me ever be put to shame" (Ps 31:1). Lord, I will no longer rely on my own strength. You are my hope. I know that I am weak, but you through Holy Communion will make me strong. "I can do all things through him who strengthens me" (Phil 4:13).

Forgive, O Jesus, all the sins I have committed against you. I repent of them with all my heart and I resolve to die rather than offend you again. I trust that in your goodness you will hear my prayer and help me to persevere in your grace until the end of my life.

Mary, my dear Mother, again with Saint Bonaventure I shall say to you also: "In you, my Lady, I seek refuge; do not let me ever be put to shame." Amen.

MEDITATION VIII

Preparation For and Thanksgiving After Holy Communion

Someone has asked why so many people who receive Holy Communion often make so little progress in the way of holiness. The answer is that it is not the fault of the food received, but of the person receiving it. Basically, it is because there is a lack of preparation on the part of the recipient. History shows that the saints derived great profit from their Holy Communions, because they took great care to prepare themselves well for this great privilege.

In our own preparation for Holy Communion, we should have two important goals in mind. The first is that we should try to become detached from created things, and instead fix our attention on God and on the things of God. Even though we might be in the state of grace, if our heart and mind are occupied with earthly concerns, there will be less room in us for divine love. Saint Gertrude once asked our Lord what kind of preparation she should make before receiving Holy Communion. He answered: "I ask only that you receive me thinking solely of me and not of yourself."

Our second aim in receiving Holy Communion should be to have a great desire to love Jesus more. A holy writer once stated that at this banquet those who are most hungry are the ones who are most satisfied. For this reason Saint Francis de Sales declared that the main purpose we should have in receiving Holy Communion is to advance in divine love. "We should receive Jesus out of love, for it is out of pure love that he gives himself to us."

After receiving this sacrament of love, we should spend some time in thanksgiving. There are no prayers dearer to God than the prayers we say after Holy Communion. This is a very precious time which we should use to make acts of love and offer other prayers. Our acts of love after receiving Holy Communion have more value and greater merit because they are imbued with the spirit of Jesus, who is then within us.

Saint Teresa of Ávila says that after we receive Communion Jesus remains within us as if seated on a throne of grace saying to us: "What do you want me to do for you? I am come down from heaven just to give you graces. Ask me for whatever you want, as much as you want, and you will be heard."

O, what treasures of grace are lost by those who spend only a short time praying to God after they receive Holy Communion!

Affections and Prayers

O God of love, you desire so much to grant us your favors, and yet we do not even seem to want to receive them. What sorrow shall we feel at the hour of death, when we remember how we were so negligent and careless. O Lord, I ask you now to forget my negligence of the past. For the future, I will prepare myself better for Holy Communion by trying to detach myself from everything that might prevent me from receiving the bountiful graces you wish to bestow upon me. And then, after receiving this Holy

Sacrament, I will lift up my heart to you in every way I can, in order that I may have your help and advance in your love.

My Jesus, may I spend the rest of my life preparing myself for death and making amends for the offenses I have committed against you. I love you, Jesus my love. Have pity on me and do not forsake me ever.

And you, my dear Mother Mary, do not cease to help me by your intercession. Amen.

Chapter Four

A CHRISTMAS NOVENA

MEDITATION I: DECEMBER 16

God Has Given Us His Only Son to Save Us

"I will give you as a light to the nations,
that my salvation may reach to the
end of the earth" (Isa 49:6).

Consider that the Eternal Father spoke these words to the Infant Jesus at the very instant of his conception in Mary's womb: "I will give you...to the nations that my salvation may reach to the end of the earth." My Son, I give you to the world for the light and life of all peoples, in order that you may bring them salvation. I desire their salvation as much as if it were my own. For this reason, you must give yourself up entirely for their sake.

This means, then, the Father went on to say, that you will have to suffer extreme poverty at the time of your birth in order that all peoples may become rich, for you will enrich them by your own indigence. This means, too, that you will be treated as a slave that they may become free. It means, also, that you will be scourged and crucified, made to suffer in their place and atone for the punishment due to them because of their sins.

In short, you will live not for yourself but for them, so that in you will be fulfilled the prophecy of Isaiah: "For a child has been born for us, a son is given to us" (Isa 9:6). In this way, my Son, they will be forced to love me and to belong to me, when they see that I am giving you, my only begotten Son, to them and when they realize that I have nothing more precious to give to them. "For God so loved the world that he gave his only Son, so that everyone who believes in him may not perish but may have eternal life" (Jn 3:16).

The Infant Jesus, far from being saddened by the Father's proposal, was not only pleased by it, but lovingly accepted it, and was in fact delighted by it. "Like a strong man (he) runs its course with joy" (Ps 19:5). From the very first moment of his existence as man, the Word was willing to give himself over to save the human race by embracing all the sorrows and shame which the Redeemer would have to suffer for love of us. As Saint Bernard would later say, these were the hills and mountains over which our Savior had to cross in order to save us. "Look, he comes, leaping upon the mountains, bounding over the hills" (Song 2:8).

Consider how the Eternal Father, when he sent his only Son to be our Redeemer and the mediator between himself and us, has also in a way bound himself to forgive us as well as to love us, because of his covenant to accept us once the Son had made satisfaction for us. At the same time the Son, in accepting the plan of the Father to redeem us, has also bound himself to love us. He, then, does love us, not because of any merit on our part, but rather that he might fulfill the will of his loving Father.

Affections and Prayers

My dearest Jesus, if it is true that ownership is acquired by gift, then you are truly mine since the Father has given you to me. You were indeed born for me; you were given to me. As Scripture says: "For a child has been born for us, a son given to us" (Isa 9:6). Therefore, I can justly say to you; my God and my all!

And since you are mine, everything that belongs to you is also mine. Again I am assured of this by the words of the Scriptures: "He who did not withhold his own Son, but gave him up for all of us, will he not with him also give us everything else?" (Rom 8:32). Therefore, your precious blood is all mine, your merits are mine, your grace is mine, your paradise is mine, and since you are mine, who can ever take you away from me?

To this question the Abbot Anthony happily replied: "No one can take God away from me." With these very same words will I likewise joyfully proclaim this truth from this day forward. I know, dear Savior, that only through my own fault could I lose you or separate myself from you. Alas, I have done this in the past, but now I repent of it with my whole heart, and I am resolved to lose my life and everything I have rather than lose you again.

Eternal Father, I thank you for having given Jesus to me, and since you have done this for me, I in turn give myself entirely to you. For the sake of your Son, accept me and bind me with the chains of love so firmly that I may always be able to say: "Who will separate us from the love of Christ?" (Rom 8:35). What values shall I ever find in this world that will cause me to leave Jesus?

My Savior, since you are all mine, know that I am all yours. Do with me, and with all that I have, as you please. And Mary, my Mother, guard me with you gracious protection. Help me to be faithful to Jesus all the days of my life. Amen.

MEDITATION II: DECEMBER 17

The Distress of the Heart of Jesus in the Womb of His Blessed Mother

"Sacrifices and offerings you have not desired, but a body you have prepared for me" (Heb 10:5).

Consider the great sorrow and deep distress that must have filled the heart of the Infant Jesus when, in the very first moments of his existence in his mother's womb, his Eternal Father revealed to him all the contempt, the agony, and the many sufferings he was going to suffer on earth in order to save us from the punishments due to sin. It would be as the prophet Isaiah would later predict: "Morning by morning he wakens—wakens my ear…and

I was not rebellious, I did not turn backward. I gave my back to those who struck me, and my cheeks to those who pulled out the beard; I did not hide my face from insult and spitting" (Isa 50:4–6).

"Morning by morning he wakens my ear." This means, says Jesus, that from the very first moment of my conception, the Father made me understand that his will was that I lead a life of sorrows, and at the end die on the cross. "And I was not rebellious…. I gave my back to those who struck me." Oh my people, I accepted all this suffering for your salvation and was willing to give my body over to the scourgers, and to those cruel men who would nail me to the cross.

Thus it is proper to say that all that Jesus was to suffer during his life and especially in his death was made known to him while he was in Mary's womb. And at the same time it is equally true to say that he accepted it all with delight, somehow overcoming the natural repugnance of the senses to suffering, but still feeling in his innocent heart the deepest anguish and oppression.

The Eternal Word knew what his earthly life would be, and what he would have to endure. First of all, after nine months in the dark prison of Mary's womb, he would be born in a poor, bare, cold stable built for beasts. Afterwards, for thirty years he would live a humble life in a carpenter's shop. At the end of his public life he would be taken captive by his enemies and treated as a slave, a false prophet, a liar, and a blasphemer worthy of death. Finally, he would be subjected to the most painful and infamous death, the kind reserved for the most worthless of criminals.

Our most loving Redeemer accepted all these sufferings as they happened to him in his life on earth. But even more, when he accepted them from the very start of his earthly existence, he felt all the pains and humiliations that he would later physically endure. The knowledge that he had a divine dignity made him feel still more deeply the insults and injuries which he would receive from those he had come to save. "All day long my disgrace is before me, and shame has covered my face" (Ps 44:15).

Our loving Jesus always had before his eyes the shame he would come to endure, especially when he would be stripped naked and scourged before many onlookers, and when he would be suspended by three nails on a cross, and end his life hearing the insults and curses of the very people he had come to save. He "became obedient to the point of death—even death on a cross" (Phil 2:8). And why? For what? To save us miserable and ungrateful sinners!

Affections and Prayers

O my Jesus, how much did it cost you, even from the very first moment of your earthly existence, to deliver me from the ruin which I brought on myself by my sins? You consented to be treated as the worst and lowest of slaves in order to free me from my slavery to sin and the devil. Still, even though I knew this, I boldly continued to hurt your loving heart.

Since you, O Lord, have accepted such a painful life and an even more painful death, I now declare that out of love for you I want to accept every pain, every misery, every difficulty that may come into my life in the future. I accept them as coming from your hands, knowing that these are the hands that were once pierced by nails to deliver me from hell.

O Lord my God, give me your holy love, for your love will make all sufferings sweet and pleasant to me. I want to love you above everything. I want to love you with my whole heart. I want to love you more than myself. During your life on earth, how many great proofs of your love have you given me; yet up to now, how long have I lived in this world without offering you any sincere proofs of my love for you! O my Jesus, I am sorry for this, and I pray for your divine forgiveness.

Mary, my Mother, recommend me to your Son, for the love you bear to him. Remember that I am one of those sheep for whom your Son has died. Amen.

MEDITATION III: DECEMBER 18

Jesus Made Himself a Child to Gain Our Confidence and Our Love

*"For a child has been born for us,
a son given to us" (Isa 9:6).*

Consider that, after so many centuries of waiting, after so many prayers and sighs of longing, the Messiah finally arrived. He whom the holy patriarchs and prophets were not worthy to see, he who was the desire of the nations, "the desire of the eternal hills," came into the world. He was born into the world, and gave himself entirely to us: "A child has been born for us, a son given to us."

The Son of God made himself little to make us great. He gave himself to us that we might give ourselves to him. He came to show us his love that we might respond to it by giving him ours. Therefore, let us receive him with affection, let us love him and turn to him in all our needs.

Saint Bernard once said that children by nature "give easily." For this reason Jesus came into the world as a child, in order to show that he was ready and willing to give us all good gifts. In the Sacred Scriptures we find Saint Paul saying that in Christ "are hidden all the treasures of wisdom and knowledge" (Col 2:3). In these same Scriptures, Saint John reminds us: "The Father loves the Son and has placed all things in his hands" (Jn 3:35).

If then we wish for light, Jesus has come to enlighten us. If we wish for strength to overcome our enemies, Jesus has come to give us peace and security. If we wish for pardon and salvation, Jesus has come to forgive and save us. If indeed we wish for the greatest gift of all, divine love, Jesus has come to fill and inflame our hearts with this grace. Note that he has come as a little child in order to show himself to us as lovable, worthy of our love. As a little child he will more easily win our affections, and in no way cause us to be afraid. As Saint Peter Chrysologus tells us: "He has come in such a way as to drive away our fears and seek our love."

Jesus then has come to us as a little child to make us love him, not just out of gratitude, but rather with a special kind of tenderness. Infants by their very nature attract the tender affection of the people who come into contact with them. So who can possibly not love, and in the most tender manner, a God whom they see as a infant needing to be nursed, an infant trembling with cold, an infant helpless and poor, rejected by all save his mother and foster father, an infant lying on a bed of straw?

It was this vision that made Saint Francis exclaim: "Let us love the child of Bethlehem, let us love the child of Bethlehem." Come, then, you who read these words, love a God who has become a poor infant, yet who is so totally lovable and charming, and has come down from heaven to give himself entirely to you.

Affections and Prayers

O my loving Jesus, we have treated you with so much coldness, and yet you have come to our earth to save us and to give yourself entirely to us. How can we have so often turned our backs on you? We do not do this to other people. If anyone gives us anything, if anyone comes from any distance to visit us, if anyone shows us any kind of affection, we do not forget this. Furthermore, we feel obliged to show them our deepest gratitude. And yet, we are so ungrateful to you, who have done so much for us, and have even given us your love and your life.

Sad to say, I myself have been worse than others in the way I personally have treated you, despite the fact that I have been so much more loved by you than they have been. If you had given these same graces to an unbeliever, or to a heretic, he or she would have become a saint. Yet I have continued to offend you. O my Savior, forgive the offenses I have committed against you. Remember that you have promised that when a sinner repents you will no longer remember his sins. "None of the transgressions they have committed shall be remembered against them" (Ezek 18:22).

If in the past I have not loved you, in the future I will do nothing else but love you. You have given yourself entirely to me, now I give you my whole will, my whole self. I love you, I love you, and I hope to continually repeat these words during the rest of my life and at the moment of my death: My God, I love you.

Mary, my Mother, you are the Mother of perseverance, obtain for me this great grace, the grace of perseverance until death. Amen.

MEDITATION IV: DECEMBER 19

The Sufferings of Jesus Lasted Throughout His Entire Life

"How long must I bear pain in my soul, and have sorrow in my heart all day long?" (Ps 13:2).

Consider again that at the very first moment of his existence in Mary's womb, the infant Jesus knew that he was to die for the redemption of the entire human race. At the same time he knew what sufferings he would have to endure, even unto death, to accomplish our redemption.

These sufferings would accompany his entire life. They would be part of the hard labor, the insults, the poverty he would come to know in Bethlehem, in Egypt, and even in Nazareth. They would include especially the unspeakable sufferings of his passion and death, the scourging, the thorns, the crucifixion, and all the untold agony and sadness, even the abandonment he would feel as he ended his earthly life on the cross of Calvary.

When Abraham was taking his son, Isaac, up the mountain to offer him in sacrifice, he did not tell him beforehand what was going to happen, even though the journey would be but a short one. But the Eternal Father chose that his own only begotten Son, who was destined to be the victim in atonement for our sins, should know even from the first moments of his existence the sufferings that awaited him. These were the very mortal sufferings of which Jesus spoke in the Garden of Gethsemane, when he stated: "I am deeply grieved, even to death" (Mt 26:38).

Our blessed Redeemer's entire life, then, was one of pains and tears. Jesus could say as did the psalmist: "For my life is spent with sorrow, and my years with sighing" (Ps 31:10). His sacred heart did not pass one moment free from suffering. Whether awake or asleep, whether at work or at rest, whether praying or preaching, he constantly had before his eyes the picture of the torments awaiting him, torments which were greater than the sufferings of all the holy martyrs. The martyrs suffered much, it is true; but they suffered with joy and enthusiasm. Jesus suffered, but with a weary and sorrowful heart. Yet he accepted everything for love of us.

Affections and Prayers

O my sweet and loving Jesus, even from your infancy you suffered, without consolation and without relief. You suffered in order to satisfy for the eternal sorrow and eternal agony in hell which I have merited because of my sins, and because I have boldly turned my back on my God.

I thank you profoundly, O afflicted heart of my Savior. I thank you and I sympathize with you, especially when I see that even though you have suffered for us, so many of us do not even pity you. O great love on the part of God! O great ingratitude on our part! How few there are who remember your sufferings and sorrows, how few who truly love you!

Unhappy me, for I have lived so many years seemingly unaware of your love. Forgive me, my Jesus, forgive me for I now intend to amend my life and love you. With your help I will not resist your grace again, I will no longer be unmindful of your love. Give me light, give me strength, to fulfill your will from now on. Grant this my prayer through the merits of your own passion and death.

And you Mary, my dearest Mother, help me. It is you who have obtained for me all the favors I have received from God. I bless you for them, but if you do not continue to help me, I will be as faithless in the future as I have been in the past. Amen.

MEDITATION V: DECEMBER 20

From the Beginning, Jesus Offered Himself for Our Salvation

"He was oppressed, and he was afflicted, yet he did not open his mouth" (Isa 53:7).

Our divine Savior, from the very first instant of his existence in his mother's womb, offered on his own accord to suffer and die in order to redeem us. The prophet Isaiah spoke at length about how "the suffering Servant of God" would be wounded for our transgressions, how he would bear our infirmities, how he would be crushed for our iniquities, and yet would not open his mouth. (See Isaiah, chapter 53.)

Jesus knew that all the sacrifices of goats and bulls offered to the Father in Old Testament times could not satisfy for the sins which had been, or later would be, committed against God. He knew that there was need for a divine Person to accomplish the redemption of the human race. This was indeed revealed in the Scriptures: "When Christ came into the world he said, 'Sacrifices and offerings you have not desired, but a body you have prepared for me….' Then I said: 'See, God, I have come to do your will, O God'" (Heb 10:5, 7).

So then we can hear Jesus saying to the Father: "My Father, all the sacrifices which have been until now offered to you have not been enough, nor will they ever be enough, to satisfy your justice. Now you have given me this human body which is capable of suffering, so that by suffering and by shedding my blood, I will appease you and redeem the human race.

See, I have come to do your will, I am ready, I accept whatever you will."

Jesus was fully human so without a doubt he naturally felt repugnance at the thought of suffering and of dying, especially the kind of death so painful and full of shame as he was destined to experience. But at the same time he was able to understand perfectly and accept totally the Father's will, even though this meant that he would begin from that moment on to suffer, at least interiorly, the anguish and pains of his crucifixion and death.

That was the way Jesus reacted. But how do we react? How have we acted toward Jesus since the time when we as adults have known, through the light of faith, about the saving mysteries of our own redemption? What thoughts have filled our minds? What plans have we made for our own eternity? What treasures have we stored up? What pleasures have we sought after? In short, where is our heart?

If we truly are guided by faith, we must finally strive to change our life and our loves. Let us then love a God who has loved us so much. Let us recall again and again the sufferings which the heart of Jesus has endured for us, even from his infancy. If we do, then we shall be unable to love anything else than the heart which has loved us so much.

Affections and Prayers

My gracious Lord, how badly I have behaved toward you during so much of my life! I have so often despised your love and your grace. You know this far better than I, and yet you have put up with me because you love me so much. Even when I tried to flee from you, you pursued me and called out to me. The same love which you had for me when you came down from heaven has made you search for me as one of your lost sheep.

My Jesus, you are looking for me and now I want to be found by you. Finally I am searching for you and I know that your grace is helping me do this. Yes, your grace is helping me to have a deep sorrow for my sins, as well as a great desire to love you and please you as much as I can. Even though I feel afraid at the thought of my own weakness, I trust in your grace and mercy, as well as your merits and love. I feel that I can say along with your apostle Paul: "I can do all things through him who strengthens me" (Phil 4:13).

Eternal Father, for the sake of Jesus, accept my love. If I have offended you, let the tears of the Infant Jesus who is praying for me appease your anger. "Look on the face of your anointed" (Ps 84:9). I do not deserve favors, but your innocent Son does, and he is offering you a life of suffering that you may be merciful to me.

Mary, Mother of mercy, do not cease to intercede for me. You know how much I trust in you because I know that you will never forsake those who have recourse to you as I do now.

MEDITATION VI: DECEMBER 21

Jesus, a Prisoner in His Mother's Womb

*"I am like those who have no help, like those
forsaken among the dead" (Ps 88:4–5).*

Consider that even the life which Jesus led in the womb of his mother was bitter and unpleasant for him. It was like being confined in a dark prison for nine long months. Other infants go through the same experience, but without understanding what is happening. Jesus did understand because from the first moment of his existence he had the perfect use of reason. He also possessed his senses, even though he could not use them. He had eyes, but he could not see; he had a tongue, but he could not speak; he had hands but could not use them, feet but he could not walk. So for nine months he was like a dead man shut up in a tomb. "I am become as a man without help, free among the dead."

He was indeed free, but of his own free will he had made himself a prisoner of love. It was love that deprived him of his liberty; it was love that bound him as tightly as though he was in chains, unable to move. Saint Ambrose commented on this situation: "Free among the dead! What great patience was shown by our Savior!"

Yet, even though we speak of the Infant Jesus as a prisoner in Mary's womb, it was not an unjust prison, because he was there out of love for us. He was innocence itself, but he had voluntarily undertaken to pay for our debts and satisfy for our crimes. Because of this, he became a victim of divine justice.

Behold then, the state to which the Son of God reduces himself for love of us! He, as it were, enchains himself to free us from the bonds of hell. How grateful should we not be for his love and goodness, and how deeply should we not love him in return. Out of love he has offered to pay and, in fact, has paid dearly for our sins. "Do not forget the kindness of your guarantor, for he has given his life for you" (Sir 29:15).

Affections and Prayers

"For he has given his life for you." Yes, my Jesus, the prophet is right in telling me not to forget the immense favor you have done for me. I am the criminal, you are the innocent one. But you chose to make amends for my sins by your sufferings and death. Yet, despite all your goodness I have often forgotten what you have done for me, and have even turned my back on you.

My dear Redeemer, if in times past I have forgotten your mercies, now and for the future I will never forget them again. I will remember constantly what you have done for me, and especially the love you have shown me. I am sorry that I have made such bad use of the freedom you gave me, and I again dedicate this great gift entirely to you. I ask you to bind me once again by your holy love, so that I may never again be separated from you.

Eternal Father, by the imprisonment of the infant Jesus in the womb of Mary, deliver me from the chains of sin and hell.

And you, my most dear Mother Mary, since Jesus remains in a sense your prisoner still, he will do everything you tell him to do. Tell him then to pardon me; tell him to make me holy. Amen.

MEDITATION VII: DECEMBER 22

The Sorrow Our Ingratitude Has Caused Jesus

"He came to what was his own, and his own people did not accept him" (Jn 1:11).

At Christmastime in Assisi, the normally happy Saint Francis used to walk about the town sad-faced and sorrowful. When he was asked why he was sad, he replied: "How can I not weep when I see that love is not loved. I see a God who became, as it were, a fool for love of us, and yet we remain so ungrateful." If our ingratitude so afflicted the heart of Saint Francis, how much more must it have affected the heart of our Lord and Savior, Jesus.

He was hardly conceived in the womb of Mary when he already perceived how he would be received. He descended from heaven to bring to earth the fire of divine love as he himself proclaimed: "I came to bring fire to the earth, and how I wish it were already kindled" (Lk 12:49). Instead, he saw the multitude of sins which we would commit even after witnessing the many proofs of his love. It was this, says Saint Bernardine of Siena, which made him feel profound sorrow.

In our own relationships with one another, ingratitude can cause many broken hearts. Blessed Simon of Cassia remarked that those who are ungrateful hurt us much more than those who inflict physical pain upon us. What feelings of sorrow, then, I ask, must have afflicted the heart of Jesus, our divine Savior, in seeing that his love and his sacrifices would be repaid by coldness and indifference on our part. "So they reward me evil for good, and hatred for my love" (Ps 109:5).

Even in our own day, it seems that Jesus has a right to complain in the words of the psalmist: "I have become a stranger to my kindred" (Ps 69:8). For he readily sees that many people neither know nor love him. They act as if he had done nothing for them, that he has not even suffered for them. Jesus once appeared to Blessed Henry Suso as a pilgrim going from door to door, begging for lodging, but everyone drove him away harshly, and with insults. It was like the scene from Job: "They said to God, 'Leave us alone,' and 'What can the Almighty do to us?' Yet he filled their houses with good things" (Job 22:17–18).

If in the past we have spoken so ungratefully to our loving God, does that mean we must continue to do so? Not at all, for our loving Savior in no way deserves our ingratitude. He came down from heaven to suffer and die for us; now we must love him in return.

Affections and Prayers

O my Jesus, is it true that you came down from heaven to make me love you? Is it true also that you embraced a life of suffering and death on the cross for my sake? Is it true that you did this in order that I might welcome you into my heart, and yet I have so often driven you away by my sins? O dear God, if you were not infinite goodness, if you had not given up your life for me, I would never have the courage to ask for pardon. But I feel that you offer me pardon and peace: "Return to me, says the LORD of hosts, and I will return to you" (Zech 1:3).

You, O Lord, have made yourself our intercessor. "If anyone does sin, we have an advocate with the Father, Jesus Christ the righteous; and he is the atoning sacrifice for our sins" (1 Jn 2:1–2). I will not insult you again by not trusting in your mercy. I repent with all my heart for having offended you and with your grace I will never drive you away again by sin.

Mary, my Queen and my Mother, pray to Jesus for me; make me live the rest of my days in this world grateful to the God who has loved me so much even after I have so greatly offended him. Amen.

MEDITATION VIII: DECEMBER 23

The Love Which God Has Shown to Us by the Birth of Jesus

"The grace of God has appeared, bringing salvation to all, training us to renounce impiety and worldly passions, and…to live lives that are self-controlled, upright and godly, while we wait for the blessed hope and the manifestation of the glory of our great God and Savior, Jesus Christ"
(Tit 2:11–13).

Consider that the "grace of God" which has appeared to us is really Jesus who loves us with a most tender love. His is a love which we have neither merited nor deserved, which is the reason it is called a "grace."

His love is also eternal. It has always existed, but in the Old Testament it was perhaps not always clearly evident. It was, we know, often promised through the prophets, and sometimes foreshadowed by various persons and events in the Old Testament. But it finally and definitely became crystal clear with the earthly appearance of Jesus, who as the Eternal-Word-made-man revealed God's tremendous love for us. He did this even as an infant, lying in a manger, crying and shivering in the cold midnight air. From the start of his life on earth, then, Jesus was making satisfaction for our sins, and he continued to show us his love until the very end of that life. "We know love by this, that he laid down his life for us" (1 Jn 3:16).

Why, then, have so many people failed to recognize this love in the past. Why do so many remain ignorant or unmindful of it today? The answer to these questions is found in Holy Scripture: "The light has come into the world, and people loved darkness rather than light" (Jn 3:19). People have not known him, nor do they know him today because they do not wish to know him, preferring the darkness of sin to the light of grace.

We must do all we can to avoid being in the number of these unfortunates. If in the past we have shut our eyes to the light, not remembering the love Jesus has shown for us, let us during the time left to us on earth try to meditate often on the sufferings and death of Jesus, our Redeemer. If we do this, then we will perhaps come to love him very much, but never as much as he has loved us.

The words of Scripture encourage us to do this "while we wait for the blessed hope and the manifestation of the glory of our great God and Savior, Jesus Christ" (Tit 2:13). We may await with hope, for the Father has promised us the paradise which Jesus has won for us by his life and death on earth. In his first coming, Jesus appeared as a poor and humble infant, lying in a manger in a stable fit only for beasts. But at his Second Coming, he will arrive on a throne of majesty: "They will see 'the Son of Man coming on the clouds of heaven' with power and great glory" (Mt 24:30). Blessed then will be those who have loved him, and miserable then will be those who have not.

Affections and Prayers

O my holy Infant Jesus, now I see you lying on straw, poor, afflicted, and forsaken. But I know that one day you will come to judge me, seated on a throne of majesty, and attended by angels. Please forgive me now, I beg you, before you come to judge me.

Then you will have to act as a just judge but now you are still my merciful Redeemer. Unfortunately, I have been one of the ungrateful persons who did not know you because I have deliberately chosen not to know you. Instead of being led to your love, I have thought only of satisfying my own pleasures. I have despised your grace and your love. But now into your hands I commend my soul, my entire self. "Into your hand I commit my spirit; you have redeemed me, O LORD, faithful God" (Ps 31:5).

In you, then, I place all my hopes, knowing that you have died on the cross to ransom me from hell. You did not condemn me to death when I was living in sin, but you have waited for me with infinite patience to repent of having offended you, and then to fall in love with you. Now I do repent, dear Jesus, and I ask you to forgive and save me. Let my salvation be to love you always above all things.

Mary, my dearest Mother, recommend me to your Son. Tell him that I am your servant, and that I have placed all my hopes in you. He hears you always and never refuses you. Amen.

MEDITATION IX: DECEMBER 24

Saint Joseph Goes to Bethlehem With His Holy Spouse

"Joseph also went from the town of Nazareth in Galilee to Judea, to the city of David called Bethlehem" (Lk 2:4).

The Eternal Father had determined that his Son should be born not in the house of Joseph, but in the city of David. More specifically, he was to be born in a stable in Bethlehem, in the poorest and most wretched way a child can be born. And so he caused the Roman Emperor Augustus to command all Jewish citizens to go to their home town and register there.

When Joseph learned of this order he became very disturbed. He had to make a decision on whether to take his spouse Mary, who was about to deliver her child, on the long journey to Bethlehem or to leave her at home.

We can imagine him speaking to Mary in this way: "My dear wife, I do not wish to leave you alone in your condition, yet on the other hand I do not wish to make you suffer during the long and difficult journey to Bethlehem. And you know that we cannot afford the kind of comfort you require. I don't know what to do."

But Mary answers him sweetly: "My dear Joseph, do not fear. I will go along with you and I know that the Lord will help us." She knew, both by divine inspiration, as well as from the words of the prophet Micah, that the Messiah was to be born in Bethlehem. So she gathered the swaddling clothes and whatever other garments she would need for her child, and went along with Joseph. They went to Bethlehem, the city of the house and family of David, the great king and an ancestor of Joseph.

Imagine, if you will, the many devout and holy conversations which Joseph and Mary had on the way to Bethlehem. How they must have dwelt on the mercy, the goodness, the love of their God whose Son was so soon to appear on earth for the salvation of the human race! Listen in your mind to the words of praise and benediction, the acts of thanksgiving and humility and love, which these two holy pilgrims must have recited along the way.

In her unique condition, Mary surely suffered much during so long a journey, as they trudged over the rough roads, the steep hills, in the very heart of winter. But she suffered with peace and with love. She offered to God all her pains, all her discomfort, in union with those of the Infant Jesus whom she carried in her womb.

Today as we draw near to the blessed feast of Christmas, let us ask Mary and Joseph to accompany us through the journey of our own life. And above all, let us beg the King of heaven, who was born in a stable, and who made his first appearance in the world as a tiny infant, to be always with us as we pass through life on our way to heaven. How blessed shall we be if, both in life and in death, we remain close to these three most holy persons—Jesus, Mary and Joseph—and they to us!

Affections and Prayers

My beloved Redeemer, I know that in your journey to Bethlehem you were also accompanied by hosts of angels from heaven, but except for Mary and Joseph, who else went with you? Oh my Jesus, allow me to accompany you at least in spirit. I know that I have been a miserable sinner. I know that I have been ungrateful to you. But now I see the injuries I have done to you and am so very, very sorry.

You came into this world to bring forgiveness; forgive me now. I repent with all my heart of having so often turned my back on you. Now I hope and pray never more to separate myself from you. Unite me, bind me, fasten me with the sweet strong cords of your divine love.

Mary, my holy Mother, do not ever abandon me during this my life journey which will end only in eternity. Assist me always, but especially at that moment when I shall arrive at the end of my life here on earth, so that I may live with and love Jesus and you forever in heaven. Amen.

A Meditation for Christmas Day

The Birth of Jesus

The birth of Jesus Christ is truly a cause for universal joy. He is the Redeemer, the one whose coming had been looked for, and sighed for, throughout all the centuries of the Old Testament. It was there that he was called the desired of the nations, of the everlasting hills. And now he has finally come into this world: born as an infant in a stable, a shelter for animals.

Yet at his birth the angels of heaven announced to the shepherds, as indeed they still announce to us, "Do not be afraid; for see—I am bringing you good news of great joy for all people: to you is born this day in the city of David a Savior, who is the Messiah, the Lord" (Lk 2:10–11).

In countries where kings still rule, what great joy abounds when an heir to the throne is born. How much grander should be our joy and our celebration when we see the Son of God born into our world through the tender mercy of the Father. "By the tender mercy of our God, the dawn from on high will break upon us" (Lk 1:78). We were lost, and behold he has come to save us. As we pray in the Nicene Creed: "For us…and for our salvation he came down from heaven."

He is also the Good Shepherd who came to save his sheep. "I am the good shepherd. The good shepherd lay down his life for the sheep" (Jn 10:11). Behold then the Lamb of God who came to sacrifice himself, to win the Father's favor for us, to become our deliverer, our life, our light, and even our food in the Holy Eucharist.

Saint Maximus observes that it was for this reason among

others that Jesus chose to be laid in a manger, which is a kind of box from which animals get their food. This was, says the saint, to make us understand that he became man to become our food: "His own body would be our eternal food." And now we can also say that every day he is born again in the sacrifice of the Mass, where the altar becomes a kind of crib.

Some people, upon reading the story of the presentation of Jesus in the Temple, might wish to have the same privilege that the aged Simeon had, that of holding the child Jesus in his arms. We should remember, however, that when we receive Holy Communion the same Jesus who was born in Bethlehem is present not only in our arms but in our very selves. This is why he was born, to give himself entirely to us. "For a child has been born for us, a son given to us" (Isa 9:6).

Affections and Prayers

The psalmist wrote: "I have gone astray like a lost sheep; seek out your servant" (Ps 119:176). Lord, I am that sheep. By following my own pleasures and desires, I have become miserably lost. But you, who are both sheep and shepherd, came down from heaven to save me. "Here is the Lamb of God who takes away the sin of the world!" (Jn 1:29).

Therefore, dear Lord, if I desire to amend my life, why should I fear? Why should I not entirely trust in you who were born to save me. "Surely God is my salvation; I will trust, and will not be afraid" (Isa 12:2). What greater proof do I have of your mercy than your very self among us? What more can inspire me with confidence than to know that you came to save me?

I know that in the past I have grieved you by my sins, but since you have come to seek me, I throw myself at your feet. And even though I see you humbled and afflicted on a manger bed in Bethlehem, I acknowledge you as my Lord and my God. I feel that your infant cries and your baby tears invite me to love you; they demand my heart. Behold it, then, my Jesus, I offer it to you today. Change it and inflame it with holy love for you.

I hear you say to me from the manger: "You shall love the Lord your God with all your heart" (Mt 22:37). And I answer: My Jesus, if I do not love you who are my Lord and my God, whom shall I love? You are all mine, and now shall I refuse to be entirely yours? No, Lord, now I love you with my whole heart. I beg you to take hold of me on this holy Christmas day, and never let me go.

Mary, Mother of your newborn Son, I pray that by the consolation and joy which you felt the first time you saw and kissed your baby, ask him now to receive me as his servant and to keep me always in his holy love. Amen.

Chapter Five

MEDITATIONS FOR THE
SEVEN PRINCIPAL FEASTS
OF OUR BLESSED LADY

MEDITATION I
FEAST OF THE IMMACULATE CONCEPTION
(December 8)

It was very fitting that all three Persons of the Holy Trinity should be involved in preserving Mary free from all sin, even original sin.

This is true, first of all, in the case of God the Father since Mary is his firstborn daughter. The Son of God, Jesus, is "the firstborn of all creation" (Col 1:15), and Mary who was to become the Mother of Jesus, was destined to be the firstborn daughter of the Father by adoption. It was for this reason that God possessed her totally by his grace. "The LORD created me at the beginning of his work, the first of his acts of long ago" (Prov 8:22). Therefore, for the very honor of his Son it was fitting that the Father should preserve the Mother from all stain of sin.

Again it was highly appropriate that the Father preserve Mary from sin because she was destined to crush the head of the devil who had deceived our first parents in paradise. In Genesis 3:15, we read: "I will put enmity between you and the woman, and between your offspring and hers." Thus the Father could never allow either this "woman" or her "offspring" ever to be enslaved by the devil. In addition to this, the "woman" who was Mary, was destined to become the defender and friend of sinners. For this reason, also, it was proper for God to preserve her from sin in order that she might not appear at any time to be guilty of the same faults as those for whom she was to intercede.

Second, it was fitting that God the Son should have as a mother a woman who was totally sinless. The Son himself chose Mary as his mother. It would be ridiculous, even impossible, to believe that a person who could have a queen for a mother would choose a slave instead. How, then, can we imagine that Jesus, the Eternal Word, who could have as a mother someone who was immaculate and always a friend of the Father, would instead accept one who had been defiled in any way by sin, or one who had been an enemy of his Father?

Moreover, as an ancient author wrote, "the flesh of Christ is the flesh of Mary." Jesus as Son of God would have been horrified to have been born of even such a holy person as Saint Agnes, or Saint Cecilia, or even Saint Teresa, for even these saints (just as all the rest of us) have been defiled by sin before their baptism. But since Mary was always pure and always free of all sin, Jesus, the second Person of the most holy Trinity, would feel no revulsion or fear in becoming man in her chaste womb.

Third, it was fitting that the most beloved spouse of God the Holy Spirit should be immaculate. The people of the Old Testament who in life sinned were nevertheless destined to be redeemed some day. But, at the same time, it was more proper that the Mother of the Redeemer and the loving spouse of the Spirit should be redeemed earlier and in a special way by being preserved from any type of sin. Then, too, if we believe (and we do) that God preserved the body of Mary after her death, how much more should we believe that at her conception he preserved her soul from the corruption of sin?

This is why in the Song of Songs, the Holy Spirit speaks of "a garden locked, a fountain sealed" (Song 4:12) because no enemy ever entered the blessed soul of Mary. For this reason, too, in the same passage God salutes her in these words: "You are altogether beautiful, my love; there is no flaw in you" (Song 4:7).

Oh, most beautiful Lady, I rejoice in seeing you so dear to God because of your purity and beauty. I thank God for having preserved you from every stain of sin. And since you are so loved by the Holy Trinity, do not refuse to look with love upon me, a sinner. Obtain for me from God pardon for my sins and eternal salvation. Look down upon me and change me. Draw my heart to you so that from now on I may truly love your Son and you. You know that I have placed my hopes in you, my dear Mother, so do not abandon me. Help me in life through your powerful intercession, and come to my aid especially at the hour of my death. Grant that I may die loving you and invoking your help, so that I may love you forever in heaven.

MEDITATION II
THE FEAST OF THE PURIFICATION[3]
(February 2)

Forty days after the birth of Jesus, it was time for Mary to be purified in the Temple. This was in accord with Jewish law. It was also the time for her to present Jesus to the Eternal Father, also mandated by Jewish law.

So, accompanied by Joseph, Mary went to the Temple in Jerusalem, carrying her divine son as well as two turtledoves which were to be offered to the Lord. Note that she offered Jesus as the true Lamb of God, and as a token of the great sacrifice which he would one day accomplish on the cross of Calvary.

O my God, I on my part unite my sacrifice to that of Mary. I offer to you your own divine Son, and by his merits I ask you to grant me all the graces I need for salvation. I do not deserve them, but I know that Jesus sacrificed himself on the cross to obtain them for me. For the love of Jesus, then, have mercy on me.

Consider how Mary entered the Temple, and in the name of the entire human race, offered up her Son. At the same time, Jesus made an offering of himself to his Eternal Father. "Behold me," he said to the Father, "I consecrate my entire life to you. You have sent me into this world to save it; accept then my blood and my life. I offer them without reserve to You for the salvation of the whole world."

---

3. This feast is also known as the Presentation of Jesus in the Temple.

How unfortunate it would have been for me, my Savior, if you had not satisfied divine justice for me! I thank you with my whole soul, and I love you with my whole heart. Indeed, whom should I love if I do not love a God who has sacrificed his life for me?

The sacrifice which Jesus made was more precious in the eyes of God than if all the human beings and all the angels had offered to God their own lives. Through this precious and priceless sacrifice on the part of Jesus, the Eternal Father received infinite honor and infinite satisfaction. Referring to this, Jesus one day said to the holy woman, Angela de Foligno: "I offered myself for you so that you might offer yourself to me."

Yes, my Jesus, because you have offered your life to the Father for love of me, I do now offer my life and my entire self to you. Up till now I have been so ungrateful, and have even made light of your supreme gift. Still you have promised that you would not remember the failures of the sinner who repents of having offended you. My Jesus, I do repent. I wish that I could die of grief. I was dead through sin; but now I hope for life from you. May my life be to love you, my great and infinite good. Make me love you; I wish for nothing more. I desire only the treasure of your love.

Mary, my queen and mother, from you I hope for every grace I will need to get to heaven.

MEDITATION III
THE FEAST OF THE ANNUNCIATION
(March 25)

When God was pleased to send his Son to our earth to become man and to redeem us, he chose for his Son a Virgin Mother. Of all possible women who lived or would live on earth, this chosen woman was the most pure, the most holy, and the most humble.

We know how the story began. One day when Mary was in her own poor home, praying for the coming of the Redeemer, the angel Gabriel appeared to her and greeted her in these words: "Greetings, favored one! The Lord is with you" (Lk 1:28).

How did Mary respond to so honorable a salutation? She was not made proud by it. No, in fact she was silent and troubled, even perplexed. She "pondered what sort of greeting this might be" (Lk 1:29).

She surely did not suspect that she herself might be destined to become the mother of the Messiah. The words she heard from the angel only caused her to fear, so much so that the angel had to encourage her. This he did by saying: "Do not be afraid, Mary, for you have found favor with God" (Lk 1:30). Then he disclosed the reason for his coming: "And now, you will conceive in your womb and bear a son, and you will name him Jesus" (Lk 1:31).

O Mary, my holy Mother, blessed indeed are you. How dear you were to God, and how dear your are still to him. And also how humble you are while I am so filled with pride. Have pity on me and obtain for me a sense of humility.

Once when reading the annunciation story, Saint Bernard

commented: "And now, O holy Virgin, why do you delay your consent? The Eternal Word himself awaits to clothe himself with human flesh and become your Son! We too await it, for we would remain in misery, condemned to eternal death until you give your consent and become the Mother of Jesus who will set us free. So quickly, dear Mother, answer and delay not the salvation of the world."

But we need wait no more. Let us rejoice! Mary hears the word of the angel, and replies in her own wonderful words: "Here am I, the servant of the Lord; let it be with me according to your word" (Lk 1:38). Mary calls herself the servant of the Lord which indicates that if he still wishes to have a servant for a mother, it is something that glorifies not herself, but rather his own goodness alone. He it is who honors her.

O my most humble Mary, by your own selflessness, you won the heart of a God. You have drawn him to you so that he has become your Son and our Redeemer. I know that your Son refuses you nothing when you ask him. Ask him then to forgive me all my offenses, and to grant me perseverance until death. O Mary, you have to save me; you are my hope.

MEDITATION IV
THE FEAST OF THE VISITATION
(July 2)

After learning that she was to become the Mother of the Redeemer, Mary set out from Nazareth to visit her cousin, Elizabeth. In this journey, Mary had to travel about ninety miles to reach Elizabeth's home.

Also, it seems that the journey lasted at least seven days,

although we know from Luke's account in the Gospel that Mary wasted no time in getting to her cousin's house. "Mary set out and went with haste to a Judean town in the hill country, where she entered the house of Zechariah and greeted Elizabeth" (Lk 1:39–40).

Tell us, O holy Lady, why did you undertake such a long and difficult journey, and why were you in such a hurry? To these questions Mary will simply reply: "I went because it was my duty; I went to console members of my family."

O great Mother of God, since it is your duty to console and strengthen people with your graces, let me ask you please to visit me and console me. Your visit sanctified the home of Elizabeth; come, sweet Mother, and sanctify me also.

Let us note that when Mary arrived at the home of Zechariah and Elizabeth, even though she already knew that she had been chosen to become the Mother of Jesus, she was the first to greet her cousin. "She entered...and greeted Elizabeth" (Lk 1:40).

On her part Elizabeth, enlightened by God, also knew that Mary was going to be the Mother of the Messiah and announced this startling news by saying to Mary: "Blessed are you among women, and blessed is the fruit of your womb. And why has this happened to me, that the mother of my Lord comes to me?" (Lk 1:42–43).

And how did Mary react to these words? She replied with the utmost humility, saying: "My soul magnifies the Lord, and my spirit rejoices in God my Savior" (Lk 1:46–47). It is as if she was telling her cousin ever so gently: Ah, Elizabeth, you praise me, but I praise my God who has been pleased to exalt me, his poor servant, by giving me the dignity of becoming his

Mother. "He has looked with favor on the lowliness of his servant" (Lk 1:48).

O most holy Mother Mary, since you give God's graces to those who ask for them, I beg you to give me the grace of humility. You think of yourself as nothing before God, but I am worse than nothing, because I am a sinner. You can make me truly humble; please do so for the love of him who made you his Mother.

Let us consider what also happened when Elizabeth heard Mary's greeting. The Gospel story tells us that "when Elizabeth heard Mary's greeting, the child leaped in her womb. And Elizabeth was filled with the Holy Spirit" (Lk 1:41). Elizabeth's child, who was later to become John the Baptizer, exulted with joy because of the divine grace which was conferred on him while still in his mother's womb. Elizabeth, as we have said, was also filled with the Holy Spirit, and her husband, Zechariah, the father of John, who had been struck dumb and was unable to speak, shortly later had has voice restored.

How true it is, most holy Mary, that through you God distributes his graces and souls are sanctified. For this reason, then, my Queen and Mother, do not forget me, your servant. I love you and place all my hopes in you. Your prayers are always heard by our gracious God, who loves you so much. Hasten to me, then, dear Mary, pray for me and make me a saint.

MEDITATION V
THE FEAST OF THE ASSUMPTION
(August 15)

We believe that Mary died, as we all must die. But let us ask: how did Mary die?

First of all, we can be sure that Mary died totally detached from all created things. She died consumed, as it were, by that divine love which had inflamed her holy and loving heart during her entire life.[4]

O my most holy Mother, you have indeed left this earth. But do not forget us miserable pilgrims who remain in this valley of tears, struggling against our many enemies. They wish to see us buried in hell. By the merits of your own death, obtain for us detachment from earthly things, as well as the forgiveness of all our sins, a strong love for God, and holy perseverance until death. And when the hour of our death arrives help us from heaven with your powerful prayers. Obtain for us the grace to be with you forever in paradise.

Yes, Mary died, and her holy body was carried by the apostles and placed in a sepulcher where it was guarded by angels for

---

4. Editor's note: In writing about Mary's Assumption into heaven, Saint Alphonsus follows the popular theology of his time. Since then, the Church has made an official pronouncement on the matter. It reads as follows: "Finally, the Immaculate Virgin, preserved free from all stain of original sin, when the course of her earthly life was finished, was taken up body and soul into heavenly glory, and exalted by the Lord as Queen over all things, so that she might be the more fully conformed to her Son, the Lord of lords and conqueror of sin and death" (see Pius XII, *Munificentissimus Deus*, 1950).

three days. Then it was taken by them to heaven. But Mary's beautiful soul had already entered into the eternal kingdom. At the very moment when she expired on earth Mary was brought into heaven by innumerable angels and by her own dear Son, Jesus.

Upon her entrance into heaven, our dear Mother humbly presented herself before God himself. She adored him and thanked him for all the graces bestowed upon her in life. Then our almighty God embraced his beloved daughter, blessed her, and declared her Queen of the universe, exalted above all the angels and saints.

And if, as we read in sacred Scriptures, the human mind cannot comprehend the tremendous glory which God has prepared for his faithful servants who have loved and served him on earth, what must we say of the glory that God bestowed upon his holy Spouse, the Mother of his Son, the one who on earth loved him more than all the angels and saints, the one who loved him with all her strength and total being! For of all creatures only Mary could say to God: Lord, if on earth I did not love you as much as you deserve, at least I loved you as much as I could love you.

On this holy day, let us rejoice then with Mary for the glory with which God has filled her. Let us also rejoice for ourselves, for at the same time that Mary was made our Queen, she was also made our Advocate. And she is so compassionate an Advocate that she accepts and defends all sinners who recommend themselves to her. Also now she has so much power with God as judge that she wins all the cases and causes she defends.

O my Queen and Lady, our salvation is in your hands. If you pray for us, we shall be saved. Just tell your Son that you want us to be with you in heaven. He will refuse you nothing. That is why we ask you, who are our life and our sweetness, to pray for us now and at the hour of our death.

In the Byzantine Liturgy, for the feast of the "Dormition of Our Lady," there is this statement:

> *In giving birth you kept your virginity; in your*
> *Dormition you did not leave the world, O Mother*
> *of God, but were joined to the source of Life. You*
> *conceived the living God, and, by your prayers,*
> *will deliver our souls from death.*

MEDITATION VI
THE FEAST OF THE NATIVITY OF MARY
(September 8)

Before the birth of Mary, the world lived in the darkness of sin. But, as one holy writer put it, "when Mary was born, the dawn arose." Or, as we read in the Song of Songs, "Who is this that looks forth like the dawn, fair as the moon, bright as the sun...?" (Song 6:10).

Here on earth we all rejoice when the dawn appears, for it is the forerunner of the sun. When Mary was born there was cause for boundless joy on the earth, because she was the forerunner of Jesus, the Sun of Justice, who as the son of Mary saved us by his death on the cross.

This is precisely what the Church proclaims in the office for today's feast: "Your birth, O Virgin Mother of God, proclaims joy to the whole world, for from you arose the glorious Sun of Justice, Christ our God; he freed us from the age-old curse and filled us with holiness; he destroyed death and gave us eternal life."

The truth is that when Mary was born into this world, our own salvation, our true health, our total consolation accompanied her, because through Mary we have received our Savior.

Since Mary was destined to become the Mother of the Eternal Word, she was herself enriched by God with so many graces that at her conception her personal holiness exceeded that of all the saints and angels together. Her sanctity was of a higher order, in accord with her dignity as Mother of God.

O holy child! O child full of grace! Even though I am a miserable sinner, I salute you! You are God's own beloved, God's own delight. Have pity on me; because of my sins I have been hateful and repulsive in his sight. But you, most holy Mother, knew from the start how to capture the heart of God, so that he never has denied you anything, nor ever will he in the future. Our mighty God grants you everything you ask; pray then for me, recommend me to your Son, and I shall be saved.

Yes, when Mary was destined to be the Mother of God, she was at the same time ordained to become the mediatress between God and sinners. For this reason Saint Thomas said that "Mary received enough grace to save all people," and Saint Bernard called her "the full reservoir of grace, and of her fullness we may all receive."

O my Queen, mediatress of sinners, do your duty and intercede for me. My sins shall not prevent me from trusting in you, O great Mother of God. My confidence in you is so great that, even if my salvation would depend on me alone, I would place myself in your hands. O Mary, receive me and protect me, that is all I desire.

MEDITATION VII
THE FEAST OF THE PRESENTATION
(November 21)

According to tradition, Mary was only about three years old when she begged her parents to take her to live in the Temple. This was in accord with a promise that they had already made. So when it was time for her to go, the young Mary left her home accompanied by her parents, Saint Ann and Saint Joachim, and (again according to tradition) a whole host of angels.

Saint Germanus comments on this event in these words: "Go, O blessed virgin to the house of the Lord to await the coming of the Holy Spirit who will make you the Mother of the Eternal Word."

When the small caravan reached the Temple of Jerusalem, Mary turned to her parents, kissed them, then knelt before them and asked their blessing. Then without looking back, she went up the steps of the Temple, renounced all that the world could give her, and consecrated herself without reserve to her heavenly Father.

From then on, her life in the Temple was one continual exercise of love, as she offered herself totally to the Lord. Day by day, hour by hour, even moment by moment, she grew in grace. Her main desire was to correspond perfectly to the graces God was bestowing upon her.

In a vision given to Saint Elizabeth of Hungary, Mary herself said this: "Perhaps you think that I received grace and virtue without any effort. I want you to know that I received no graces from God without great labor, constant prayer, strong desire, and even many tears and mortifications on my part."

Thus it is correct to presume that in the Temple the young Mary prayed without ceasing. But believing, as she did, that the human race had strayed from God and was lost, she prayed most of all for the coming of the Messiah. As for herself, she prayed that she might become a servant of the blessed Jewish maiden, who according to tradition was to be chosen as mother of the Messiah. Little did she suspect that she would be the one!

O my dear Mary, beloved of God, you who pray for all, pray especially for me. From your very childhood, you consecrated yourself to God; obtain for me then the grace that, at least for the time that I still have to live, I too may live for God alone. In union with you I this day renounce all worldly things and con-secrate myself to God alone. I also offer myself to serve you always. Accept me as your servant, and obtain for me the grace to be faithful to you until death, so that I may one day praise you and your Son for all eternity in heaven.

Chapter Six

MEDITATIONS IN HONOR OF SAINT JOSEPH

INTRODUCTION: ON TRUE DEVOTION TO SAINT JOSEPH

The very example of Jesus, who sought so much to honor Saint Joseph, should encourage us also to have a deep devotion to this great saint. After his heavenly Father ceded his own rightful place to Saint Joseph, Jesus truly regarded Saint Joseph as a father, and gave him due respect and obedience. As Saint Luke describes it, "he [Jesus] was obedient to them" (Lk 2:51).

Saint Joseph, then, in caring for the holy family, was the head, and Jesus, as a child, was expected to obey him. That he did so, we have no doubt. He ate, he slept, he worked; in short, he did everything in accord with the directions of his foster father.

Saint Bridget received this information in a vision from God himself. "My Son was so obedient that when Joseph would say, 'Do this or do that,' he instantly did it." And a holy writer named John Gerson attests that Jesus often prepared the food, fetched the water, cleaned the house, in his role as an obedient son to his earthly parents.

Thus by his humility and in his actions, Jesus showed that, next to Mary, Joseph is superior in dignity to all the other saints. This prompted another early writer to say that we should pay great honor to Joseph since the King of kings wished to raise Joseph to such heights. And Jesus himself exhorted Saint Margaret of Cortona to have a great devotion to Saint Joseph because the saint had taken such good care of him in his early lifetime.

Many of our saints have accepted these directions from our Lord. Saint Teresa, for example, states her reactions in one of her books, "I do not remember having asked any favor of Saint Joseph which he did not grant. The many graces which God has given to me, and the corporal and spiritual dangers from which he has saved me, would cause great admiration to anyone. The good Lord appears to have given to other saints the power to assist us in a single sort of need; but experience shows that Saint Joseph helps us in all situations. God seems to want us to understand that just as Jesus was obedient to Saint Joseph on earth, so now in heaven he still does whatever the saint asks of him. Furthermore, I have not known anyone devoted to Saint Joseph who has not advanced in virtue. I ask that those who might not believe me in this will at least make an experiment in having devotion to this saint."

There is one special grace which we should ask from Saint Joseph, and expect to get it. It is the grace of a happy death. All of us must die some day, and we need to entrust ourselves to the care of Saint Joseph for that final, perhaps terrifying, experience here on earth.

There are three special reasons why Saint Joseph is the patron of a good death. First, Jesus loved this saint not only as a friend but also as a father, which makes Saint Joseph much more powerful than any of the other saints. Second, Saint Joseph has great power over the devils who might want to attack us at the end of our life. In return for having saved him from the murderous rage of King Herod, Jesus has given to Saint Joseph the special privilege of protecting the dying from the rage and snares of Lucifer. And third, because he himself had such a holy death in the presence of Jesus and Mary, Saint Joseph holds the privilege of obtaining for his own friends and devotees the grace of a sweet and holy death.

So, "Go to Joseph!"

MEDITATION I

The Journey to Bethlehem

*"Joseph also went from the town of Nazareth in
Galilee to Judea, to the city of David
called Bethlehem" (Lk 2:4).*

Let us consider the long and loving conversations Mary and Joseph must have had on this journey. Surely they spoke of the mercy of God evident in his sending his only Son into the world to redeem the human race. They must have talked, too, about the love which this Son must have for mankind which led him to atone for all our sins by his own suffering and death.

Consider also how painful it must have been for Joseph to be banished along with his wife from the city of Bethlehem on the very night when she was to give birth to the divine Word. And even after they had found shelter in a stable, how agonizing it must have been for him to see his holy spouse, in the last hours of her pregnancy, trembling with cold in the dead of the night.

But, then, consider how thrilled he must have been when Mary called him to her side and showed him her baby. "Come, Joseph, come and adore our infant God. See what a beautiful baby he is! Look at him, the king of the world, lying on a bed of straw! He who makes the angels burn with love, lies there trembling in the cold!"

Imagine, too, Joseph's own reaction, filled as he was with love and tenderness as he saw with his own eyes this infant who was the Son of God, as he heard the angels singing praises to their newborn King, as he beheld the stable filled with light. Surely Joseph knelt down and wept for joy, as he said: "My Lord and my God, I adore you! How great is my happiness to be the first, after your mother, to see you and to know that in this world you will be called my son. Allow me to call you my Son, and to say: My God and my Son, I consecrate myself to you. My life will no longer be my own but I will spend it only in serving you."

Finally, consider how Joseph was even more filled with joy when that very night the shepherds, invited by the angels, came to see the newborn Savior, and then later, when the Magi came from the east to adore the King who came down to earth to save his people.

Prayer

O my holy patriarch, Saint Joseph, through the pain which you felt in seeing Jesus lying in a manger, so poor, so cold, so helpless, I beg you to obtain for me a true sorrow for my sins by which I have caused this holy Infant so much distress. And through the consolations which you must have felt at the first sight of this child, who despite the difficult circumstances of his birth on earth still looked so beautiful and lovely that he captured your heart, obtain for me also the grace to love him here on earth and forever in heaven.

And you, O Mary, mother of God, recommend me to your Son and ask him to pardon me all my offenses, and to give me the grace never more to sin against him.

And finally, my dear Jesus, pardon me for the sake of Mary and Joseph. Give me the grace to see you and them one day in paradise. There I will thank you forever for having become an little infant for love of me.

MEDITATION II

The Flight Into Egypt

"An angel of the Lord appeared to Joseph in a dream, and said, 'Get up, take the child and his mother, and flee to Egypt'" (Mt 2:13).

When the Magi informed Herod that the new king of the Jews was born, this vicious ruler gave his soldiers the command to slaughter all the male children of Jerusalem and its environs. But God the Father, determined to deliver his Son from death at this time, sent an angel to tell Joseph to take the child and his mother into a neighboring land called Egypt.

Consider now how readily Joseph obeyed God's command. He raised no doubts about the time of the journey, no doubts about how they were to travel, no doubts about in what part of Egypt they were to stay. No, he prepared to set out immediately, even though the angel set no time for the departure.

He therefore went and told Mary what the angel had said, and on that very night, after collecting the tools of his trade, he set out with Mary and Jesus on a journey of some four hundred miles, mostly through the desert. He had no knowledge of the precise place where he was to go, and no guide.

Imagine how Joseph must have suffered in seeing how his loving spouse, carrying her Infant Son in her arms, had to face the desert storms, the cold and uncertain weather, and all the while fearful that Herod's soldiers might overcome and capture them. What kind of food did this holy family have for the journey? Where did they sleep? Who provided for them in any way?

Joseph, we are sure, was himself ready to undergo whatever sufferings and pain that were an essential part of the journey. These were, he felt, also a part of the Eternal Father's plan for his own Son in achieving our salvation. But his own tender and paternal heart must have been nearly broken at the sight of the divine Infant trembling and crying in the cold and the other inconveniences of the journey.

Then, too, consider all the other sufferings which Jesus, Mary, and Joseph must have undergone during the seven long years which the Holy Family spent in Egypt, living as they did amid an idolatrous and barbaric people. They had no relatives, and probably few friends, to assist them. They were poor, and as Saint Bernard has written, Joseph had to work day and night to feed and support his family, a family that contained one member who alone provides food for all the people—and all the beasts—of the earth!

Prayer

My holy protector, Saint Joseph, through the holy and prompt obedience which you have always shown to God's commands, obtain for me from Jesus the grace to obey and to do God's holy will. Obtain for me that in my own life journey into eternity, I may never forsake the company of Jesus and Mary and yours. If I ally myself with them and you, all the toils and sorrows of this life, and even death itself, will be sweet and agreeable to me.

Mary, my dearest Mother, through all the pains which you as a young mother endured in your journey to, and stay in, Egypt, obtain for me the grace to bear with patience all the crosses and petty inconveniences of life here on earth.

And you, my sweet Jesus, have mercy on me. Even as an infant you suffered so much for me; how does it happen that I, who have so often deserved hell for my sins, try to escape even the slightest suffering and pain? From this moment on, I pledge myself ready to bear all the crosses you send me. But I can do this only with the help of your grace; if you do not help me, I shall be unfaithful to you. Let me always love you, my Jesus, and let me accept whatever sufferings you send into my life.

MEDITATION III

Jesus Is Lost in the Temple

*"When the festival was ended and they started to
return, the boy Jesus stayed behind in Jerusalem,
but his parents did not know it" (Lk 2:43).*

When it was safe to return from their Egyptian exile, the three
members of the Holy Family went back to Judea. Again, an angel came to Joseph and told him to take the child and his mother
back to their home there. Commenting on this event, Saint
Bonaventure says that in his opinion the trio had a harder time
on this return journey because Jesus was then about seven years
old, and consequently was too large to be carried, and too small
to walk all the way. Thus there were many rest stops as they
traveled.

However, what we want to consider now is another important event in the life of Saint Joseph. It took place when Jesus
was some twelve years old. The gospel relates that at that time
Joseph, Mary, and Jesus made their customary annual visit to
the Temple in Jerusalem. We must remember that by now Joseph was used to being in the company of his beloved Savior,
and usually kept a close eye on him. What must have been his
distress then, when after the days of the festival were completed,
he was deprived of both the sight and company of Jesus for
three whole days! Furthermore, he had no idea of how and where
he might find him, nor (and this was the worst part) why Jesus
had left both his mother and him.

In his deep humility Joseph might have thought that it could have been because of some fault on his part. Or that he was no longer worthy to be in the company of the Savior. Or that he was no longer to be a part of Jesus' life, neither as companion nor as guardian.

To those who have placed all their love in God there is no pain greater than that which comes from the fear of possibly having offended God. During those three long days in Jerusalem, we can be sure that both Mary and Joseph could not sleep. We can be sure also that they wept continuously as they went about searching for the child Jesus. The words of sacred Scripture testify to this, for when they finally came upon Jesus in the temple, Mary revealed her deep misgivings and sorrow: "Child, why have you treated us like this? Look, your father and I have been searching for you in great anxiety" (Lk 2:48).

At the same time, we must consider how relieved Joseph must have been when Jesus was found, and how deep was his joy when he learned that Jesus had not left because of any neglect on his part, but only because Jesus himself was so totally filled with zeal for the glory of his heavenly Father.

Prayer

O my holy patriarch, Saint Joseph, you wept when you lost Jesus, but in truth you have always loved him and he has always loved you. Indeed, he has loved you so much that he chose you for his teacher and guardian. Far better would it be if you left the weeping and the sorrow to me because for the love of creatures and my own pleasures, I have so often lost my God by refusing his grace.

Dear Saint Joseph, through the merits of the pains which you suffered in losing the child Jesus, obtain for me the grace to weep for my sins. And through the joy which you felt in finding him in the temple, obtain for me the grace to find him once more in my heart, so that I may never lost him again.

And you, my holy Mother Mary, refuge of sinners, do not abandon me, but rather have pity on me. If I have offended your Son, please now help me to repent of this with my whole heart. Beg of him pardon and perseverance for me.

Finally, my sweet Jesus, if you have not yet pardoned me, do so this very day. I hate and detest all the injuries I have done to you. I love you now, and desire your graces more than anything in this world. Help me to love you always and never more offend you.

MEDITATION IV

The Happy and Holy Family of Nazareth

"Then he went down with them and came to Nazareth, and was obedient to them" (Lk 2:51).

After the joyful reunion in the Temple of Jerusalem, Mary and Joseph took the child Jesus with them to their home in Nazareth. There, as Scripture tells us, Jesus was obedient both to his mother Mary and to Saint Joseph, just as if Joseph were his true father.

What a beautiful and holy household it must have been! Their only preoccupation, their only concern, was the greater glory of

God. Their only thoughts and desires were how to please God. All their conversations revolved around how much love they and all other people should have for God, and how much love God has shown to all of us human beings, particularly by sending his only Son into the world to suffer and die in a sea of sorrows and pain for us.

However, in the Holy Family there were sorrows too. Think of the tears Joseph and Mary must have shed as they reflected with Jesus on the words of sacred Scripture which foretold his passion and death. Think of their own deep pain and sorrow in reading the prophecies of Isaiah where the prophet spoke of how the enemies of the Messiah who would so disfigure him that people would not be able to recognize him. Or when he predicted that the Savior's flesh would be torn and lacerated by the scourging at the pillar. Or when he was likened to a patient, silent lamb being led to the slaughter. Or, finally, when they read the terrible predictions about his death, how he would die hanging on a cross between two thieves.

Yet, even so, how consoling and strengthening must their support, their actions, their sentiments and their love have been to the human heart of Jesus!

Prayer

Saint Joseph, my holy patriarch, through the tears which you shed in foreseeing the sufferings of Jesus, obtain for me a constant remembrance of these sorrows. And also, through the flame of love which was enkindled in your heart as you spoke with Mary about the tragedy which awaited Jesus, obtain for me a spirit of repentance for my sins.

And you, O Mary, through your own sufferings at the time of Jesus' passion and death, obtain for me a deep sorrow for my sins.

And, finally, sweet Savior, you who have suffered so much for me, and even died for me, grant that I may never forget your excessive love. Your death is my hope. You have died for me and now I truly hope to be saved. I love you now above all things, and with my whole heart. I love you more than I love myself, and for love of you I am ready to suffer every pain. I am truly sorry for having offended you. Do not allow me to be ever separated from you again.

MEDITATION V

The Love Joseph Had for Jesus and for Mary

"When Joseph awoke from sleep, he did as the angel of the Lord commanded him; he took her as his wife...and he named him Jesus" (Mt 1:24–25).

Let us consider, first of all, the love which Joseph had for Mary, his holy spouse. It is safe to say that of all the women who ever existed, she was the most beautiful. In the spiritual order, she was more humble, more meek, more pure, more obedient, more lovable and more loving than all of angels of heaven or all other human beings, past, present, or future. For these reasons alone, she gained the affection of Joseph who was a just man, a lover of virtue.

Add to this picture the tenderness of the love which Mary

herself bore to him. Mary loved Joseph above all other creatures. At the same time, Joseph saw in Mary God's own beloved daughter, the one chosen to be the mother of God's only begotten Son.

All these were more than enough reasons to make Joseph love Mary above all others, save God.

Consider, too, how much love Joseph had for Jesus. When God chose Joseph to be the foster father of Jesus, he must certainly have placed in the human heart of Joseph a paternal kind of love, but in this case the "Father" was God and the "Son" was also God. For this reason, we can say that Joseph's love was more than merely human, like the love other fathers have for their children. The love of Joseph for Jesus was a type of superhuman love, since he knew from the angel that Jesus was not really his own child, but rather the Divine Word who had come to earth for love of the human race.

Joseph knew also that he had been especially chosen from all men to be the guardian of this person, who would later allow himself to be called "the carpenter's son." Think, then, of the love which filled his heart when he meditated on these mysteries, and also when he saw the child Jesus doing little things for him. As, for example, when he watched Jesus cleaning up around the house, or gathering twigs for the fire, or sawing or planing wood in the carpenter shop.

Picture in your mind how it was especially while Jesus was still an infant. How much love and affection Joseph must have felt when he carried the baby Jesus around in his own arms, or when he soothed him or put him to sleep. Later, as we read in the Gospel, "The child grew and became strong, filled with wisdom; and the favor of God was upon him" (Lk 2:40). Think of how delighted Joseph must have been to hear heavenly wisdom from the very mouth of Jesus! Think, too, of the loving example of true love that Jesus must have displayed for a Joseph who was still eager to learn more about God's love for us! Sometimes it happens that when people live together for a long time they become aware of one another's defects and failures. This was not the case in the holy house of Nazareth. The more Joseph conversed with Jesus the more he learned about his infinite holiness. What a wonderful period of life this must have been for Saint Joseph!

Prayer

My holy patriarch, I truly rejoice at your own happiness and goodness, and in the fact that you had the power to command, as a father, him who heaven and earth obey. Dear Saint Joseph, since a God has served you, I wish to enroll also in your service. From now on, I wish to serve you, to honor you, and to love you as my special patron. Take me under your protection, just as you did Jesus, and pray always for me. I know that Jesus obeyed your commands while on earth; how then can he refuse to grant you any request now that you are with him in heaven! Tell him, then, to pardon my sins and offenses and to inflame me with love for him.

And you, my sweet Mother Mary, through the love which Joseph had for you, take me under your patronage also and beg Jesus to accept me as his servant.

My dear Jesus, who to atone for my disobedience humbled yourself by obeying a man, grant me the grace to obey your every wish now and forever. You deserve the love of my entire heart. Forget now the injuries I have done to you, and have mercy on me. I love you, my Jesus, let me love you more and more!

MEDITATION VI

The Death of Saint Joseph

"Precious in the sight of the LORD is the death of his faithful ones" (Ps 116:15).

Consider how Joseph, after having faithfully served both Jesus and Mary as head of the holy house of Nazareth, finally arrived at the end of his life on earth. It was in that very house, then, that with Jesus and Mary both at his bedside, and with a heart filled with joy and peace, he departed this life for eternity.

The presence of such a holy spouse, as well as that of the Redeemer himself, who had allowed himself to be called Joseph's son, made his death sweet and precious. How could death be painful to him who died in the arms of life itself? Who could ever quite understand or explain the consolations, the hopes, the fires of love, the acts of resignation which were suggested to him by Jesus and Mary, and which thus filled his great soul as he prepared to leave this earth? It was with these considerations in mind that Saint Francis de Sales decided that Joseph died out of pure love for God.

Joseph had such a good death, a death sweet and calm, free from fear and misery, because he had led such a holy life. Those who offend God and thus deserve hell cannot expect to die such a good death. But not so for those fortunate people who will be protected by Saint Joseph when they come to die. Saint Joseph, to whom Jesus was obedient during life, has the power to command and drive away even the devils of hell, will comfort and shield all his clients who have asked him for this great favor.

Yes, happy the one who shall be helped by this great saint who himself died with the assistance of Jesus and Mary, and who saved the Infant Jesus from the danger of death by making a long and arduous journey into Egypt. Through these events alone Joseph has been given the privilege of being the patron of a good death, and of delivering his clients from the danger of eternal death.

Prayer

Saint Joseph, my holy protector, you rightly deserved such a holy death because you led such a holy life. I, however, must deserve an unhappy death, because my life has not been holy. But if you defend me, I shall not be lost. You were not only a great friend of my Judge; you were also his guardian and protector. If you put in a good word for me with my Judge, he will not know how to condemn me. For this reason, I chose you to be, after Mary, my principal protector and defender of my cause.

I promise to honor you every day by some special devotion, and by formally placing myself under your protection. Therefore, I now pray to you, that through your own blessed death in the presence of Jesus and

Mary, you will protect me at the hour of my own death, so that I may get to heaven where I will thank you forever, and in your company praise and love God for all eternity.

Mary, my Mother, do not ever abandon me but with your spouse assist me particularly at the hour of my death. Obtain for me the grace to breathe forth my soul invoking and loving you and your Son, Jesus.

And you, sweet Savior, who will one day be my just Judge, pardon all my offenses against you. I am sorry for them all. I have lost so many years in not loving you, but now I ask for the grace to love you during the time, be it long or short, which I have still to live on this earth. And when I die, make me die burning with love for you. I ask no other grace than that, to love you with all my strength from now on and through all eternity.

Jesus, Mary and Joseph, I give you my heart and my soul.

Jesus, Mary and Joseph, assist me in my last agony.

Jesus, Mary and Joseph, make me die in your company.

MEDITATION VII

The Heavenly Glory of Saint Joseph

"Well done, good and trustworthy slave;
you have been trustworthy in a few things,
I will put you in charge of many things;
enter into the joy of your master" (Mt 25:21).

The measure of glory given by God to his saints in heaven corresponds to the level of holiness which they achieved during their life on earth. To appreciate the sanctity of Saint Joseph, it is enough to recall what the Scriptures say of him: "Joseph, being a righteous man…" (Mt 1:19). A righteous man (or as some Bible versions have it, a just man) describes a person who possesses all virtues, because if he should lack even a single virtue he could not be called righteous or just.

So, if the Holy Spirit already called Joseph righteous when he was chosen to become the spouse of Mary, imagine how much more love and how many more virtues this holy man must have garnered from his close association with Mary, who surely offered him the perfect example of all virtues. Or again, if the mere voice of Mary was enough to make holy the infant John the Baptizer, and at the same time fill Saint Elizabeth with the Holy Spirit, how much more holiness must Joseph have acquired by his constant association with Mary during the twenty-five years or so when he lived in her company.

Consider, too, how living in the company of Jesus for so many years must have developed and increased the virtues of this holy man. Joseph surely served Jesus in many ways in the holy home of Nazareth. He must have helped him, worked for him, nourished him, comforted him. If Jesus promises a reward to those who give only a cup of water in his name, consider the graces which the Father was ready to bestow on the man who saved his only begotten Son from Herod, who provided him with food and clothing, carried him in his arms, and fathered him with so much tender love.

Again, we have every reason to believe that the life of Joseph, spent as it was in the presence of Jesus and Mary, was a continuous prayer, filled with acts of faith, hope, love, and of resignation to God's holy will. Since, as we have already pointed out, the reward of the saints in heaven corresponds to graces gained in life through prayer and good works, it is easy to imagine how great must be the glory of Saint Joseph in heaven.

For this reason, Saint Augustine likens the saints in heaven to the stars, but calls Saint Joseph the sun. And Father Francisco Suarez of the Society of Jesus says that it is totally within reason to suppose that after Mary, the Mother of Jesus, Saint Joseph surpasses all the other saints in glory and grace. And the holy writer, Saint Bernardine de Bustis, teaches that when Saint Joseph asks for graces for those who devoted to him, his prayers have almost the force of a command to Jesus and Mary.

Prayer

My holy patriarch, now that you are in heaven and near to your beloved Jesus who was subject to you while on earth, please pray for me. I must live still on earth, amid so many temptations, so many enemies to my soul, so many spiritual dangers. By the many graces which you gained by living for so long a time in the holy presence of Jesus and Mary, obtain for me the grace to be always united to God for the rest of my earthly life. Help me to resist the attacks of hell, so that I may die a good death, loving Jesus and Mary, now and throughout eternity.

Most holy virgin and my Mother, Mary, when will I no longer have to fear falling into sin? When shall I be able to embrace you and never more depart from your side? Only through your intercession will I ever have this kind of happiness and peace.

And you, my beloved Jesus, my dear Redeemer, when shall I see you face to face, and enjoy your loving presence in paradise? As long as I live here on this earth, I am in danger of losing your grace. I now pray that through the merits of Saint Joseph, your foster father, and through the protection of Mary, your Mother and mine, and above all through the graces you won for me through your own life, passion, death, and resurrection, you will never more permit me to be separated from you. Grant that after my days here on earth I may go to that heaven of love, there to possess and love you with all my strength forever more. This is my greatest hope and my deepest desire. Amen.